PHOTOGRAPHY

" Mr. Stanley Bowler has succeeded in producing a book which is not only evenly balanced, but manages to convey an amazing amount of sound practical teaching in a very pleasant and simple style.

He never loses sight of the fact that his book is a primer, and that its main intent is to interest the would-be photographer, guide his early steps and lead him on to a greater interest in the subject."

The Photographic Journal

Some Other Teach Yourself Books

———

Drawing
Drawing and Painting
Film-making
Handwriting
Mechanical Draughtsmanship
Painting for Pleasure
Perspective Drawing
Study Art
Study Sculpture

TEACH YOURSELF BOOKS

PHOTOGRAPHY

STANLEY W. BOWLER
F.R.P.S., F.R.S.A.

TEACH YOURSELF BOOKS
ST. PAUL'S HOUSE WARWICK LANE LONDON EC4

First Printed February 1940
Revised 1962
This impression 1970

ISBN 0 340 05683 5

Printed in Great Britain for The English Universities Press Ltd.,
by Richard Clay (The Chaucer Press), Ltd., Bungay, Suffolk

PREFACE

As we go through life we gather impressions and memories, but inevitably, whether grave or gay, those memories fade from our minds as further experiences claim our attention.

To this age, however, has been vouchsafed the priceless opportunity of preserving some of those happy memories of happenings and of people, in a form which is more permanent than many human lives. That is how I like to think of the simple " snap "—a link with the pleasurable past.

Every year myriads of such snapshots are made by amateur photographers, who, because of the excellencies of modern photographic materials and apparatus, secure a fair proportion of successful pictures. But, alas, many priceless records are spoiled for lack of simple technical information on the subject of making photographic pictures.

Because of this, because I feel there are many who would like to know the simple underlying principles of photography, and because I also think there are some who would like to do more with their hobby than merely press the camera button, this book has been prepared.

It starts right from the beginning and assumes that the reader sets out with little or no knowledge of the chemicals, equipment, processes and language of photography, and an endeavour has been made to set out the information in ordinary language and in a simple but clear manner.

In some cases the broad principles laid down will be susceptible of expansion, and even of amendment, when the knowledge of the reader becomes wider. I have, however, tried to make it possible for him, after reading this book, to carry out his first attempts at photography with a reasonable hope of success and with some knowledge of how things work. To assist him to further study of the subject should he be inspired to persevere, a list of books which will repay study has been included.

I should like to take this opportunity of acknowledging the great assistance which I received from Mr. George H. Sewell, F.R.P.S., in preparing both the text and the illustrations for this book.

As a final word, may I express the hope that the reader will in future obtain as much interest and satisfaction from his photographic hobby as I do, and if I am of help to him that this will indirectly repay those who have given me unstinted help and encouragement in the past.

S. W. B.

CONTENTS

LIST OF ILLUSTRATIONS

PLATES

CHAPTER I

THE CAMERA

ONE of the amusements of our forefathers was the *Camera Obscura*. It was a room without any windows, and when the door was closed it would have been pitch black inside, except for the fact that from a tiny hole in the roof came rays of light which, falling upon the whitened surface of a table-top, reproduced a picture of the outside world immediately surrounding the room.

If we reduce our room to the size of a small box, with a tiny hole at one end, and the flat surface of a plate or film at the other, we have an instrument which we call a *Camera*. The principles of this simple arrangement are the fundamental principles of every camera that is made, however elaborate it may otherwise be—a lighttight box, a hole at one end, and a flat piece of material sensitive to light at the other end on which the light rays can fall.

In the camera obscura the light was allowed to fall upon the white surface for as long as the spectators wished to observe the image. The outside world is hardly ever still—leaves rustle, people walk about, vehicles move—and the spectators could see all that movement on the screen.

In the camera, if the recorded picture is to be free from blurring and confusion, it is necessary to allow the light to enter for a time, so short that movement will not be apparent in the picture, but in sufficient quantity to be able to cause the necessary action to take place on the light-sensitive surface of the plate or film.

This is accomplished by controlling (*a*) the quantity of light passing through the hole in the

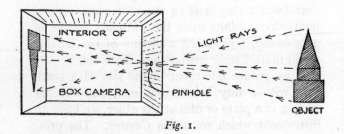

Fig. 1.

camera at any one moment, and (*b*) the period of time during which it passes.

By increasing the size of the hole in the camera the quantity of light can be made sufficient for any ordinary purposes, but, for reasons which are explained in Chapter II, it then becomes necessary to use a lens. Otherwise the picture would be indistinct. It may so happen, however, that under very bright conditions the hole is too large, and lets too much light through. A mechanism called a " diaphragm " or " stop " is then used to cut down the size of the hole. In simple cameras it takes the form of a metal plate pierced with a hole of the desired dimensions, which is placed in front of the larger hole in the camera. In more expensive instruments it is a more elaborate mechanism, known as an " iris diaphragm ", because it operates like the iris of the human eye— a round hole opening and closing at the will of the photographer. The size of the opening is known as the " aperture ".

The time during which the light passes through the hole is controlled by a shutter, which normally closes the hole, and merely uncovers it for the period required by the photographer. This is dealt with in Chapter III. In some forms of camera the hole remains open all the time, and the shutter works very close to the surface of the film or plate, protecting it from light until the time comes to take a photograph. That is known as a " focal plane shutter ", and is also dealt with in Chapter III.

HOW AN IMAGE IS FORMED. THE PINHOLE CAMERA

The simplest form of camera is the pinhole camera (probably so called because the hole at one end of the light-tight box is generally made with a *needle* through a thin sheet of metal or opaque black paper). Such a camera is shown in outline in the diagram, an examination of which will help us to understand how light from the subject draws the picture on the plate or film.

For all practical purposes, light travels in straight lines, except when it is intercepted and deliberately bent. Any object which we can see is visible because it is radiating straight lines of light from every visible point on its surface. These lines travel outwards from each point in all possible directions.

If we place our pinhole camera (as shown in Fig. 1) in front of the church, some of the rays of

Fig. 2.

light from all parts of the church will find their way to the pinhole. For example, from the pinnacle of the spire one ray will get to and through the hole and pass on to the plate or film. All the other rays from the pinnacle will be wasted as far as we are concerned, and so we will disregard them. Similar straight lines will go from all the other parts of the object, through the pinhole, on to the film, and the result will be a picture which is upside down and reversed left to right. Even when a lens is used, the principle is the same, which is the reason why the image on the back of a camera is always upside down. It is actually upside down inside our own eyes, but our minds " correct " this impression, and we see the world in normal fashion.

HOW A PHOTOGRAPH IS RECORDED

Let us look at Fig. 2, and consider how a picture is permanently recorded by the film.

Except in certain advanced processes, the film records the original subject as a black-and-white image. That is because the material with which the film or plate is coated is sensitive to the quantity of light it receives rather than the colour of it.

In our little scene the sky is very light, and the rays from it which pass through the pinhole on to the film will be brilliant and intense, and affect the film considerably. The sunlit side of the house is nearly as bright, and the rays from it will therefore cause nearly as much effect on the film. The ground and the sunlit sides of the two trees are somewhat darker, and will have even less effect on the film, whilst the shadow sides of the trees and house will have hardly any effect at all. It would be said that the *intensity* of the light rays falling upon the film varies in proportion to the intensity of the light rays being reflected from the actual subject.

If we could take the film out of the camera immediately after it had been given a controlled exposure in this way, we should be disappointed because nothing could be seen. Before the picture becomes visible, and before it is exposed to any other light (except the " safe " light of the darkroom), the film must be placed in a chemical solution called a developer. When this has acted on the film, we shall then see that where the most intense light has fallen the film will be very dark— the sky portion, for example, will be very black indeed. Where the light has been least intense— in the shadows, for example—the film will be very light. Because these darknesses, or *densities* as they are called, give just the reverse of the appearance of the actual subject, this first result is known as a *negative*. The final result, in which the light and dark values are in correct relationship and the picture looks right, is a *positive*. We are mostly familiar with the positive in the form of the *prints* or *snaps*, which so many people take. The transparent pictures produced by the colour-film processes such as Agfacolor, Ilfochrome and Kodachrome are also *positives*. Do not make the mistake which is indulged in by so many people—the fact that a picture is on a transparent support does not make it a negative, it is the nature of the image which makes it a negative, and for some purposes negatives are sometimes made on paper.

THE BOX CAMERA

The box camera is the nearest approach to the pinhole camera which you can buy. It is a plain, oblong, light-tight box. At one end, instead of a pinhole, it has a somewhat larger hole covered with a plain type of single lens, the aperture of which cannot be varied. There is a very simple shutter of the " click " type (see Chapter III.). In addition, there are some means of holding the negative material (the film or plate) in position. In earlier times box cameras for plates were made, but in these days they are practically all for roll films.

THE FOLDING CAMERA

If you cut away the front two-thirds of your rigid box and connect the front panel holding the lens to the back by a tunnel of opaque but flexible material, you can fold the camera into a smaller compass when it is not actually in use. The baseboard and struts serve to hold the lens in correct position when taking a picture. Such cameras are made for both plates and films. The simplest forms have the same types of lens and shutter as the box camera, and are a little more expensive.

The folding camera has, however, been extensively developed in design, and there is an almost bewildering variety of designs and types and prices. The underlying principles of all these instruments are the same. The advantages possessed by the more expensive cameras are :—

(a) The lenses are *faster*—that is, they have larger apertures, which allow of pictures being taken in poorer light, but require greater care in manipulation.

(*b*) It is often possible to use more than one lens on the same camera. The advantages of this are set forth in Chapter II.

(*c*) The shutter has a greater range of *speeds*—that is to say, the time during which it remains open can be varied at will, often between such widely different times as one second and one five-hundredth of a second.

(*d*) In the more elaborate up-to-date instruments some form of *range-finder* is incorporated which enables you to get your picture sharp and crisp and exactly as you want it, with certainty and the minimum of trouble.

METHODS OF LOADING

Roll-film Cameras.—The film is purchased on a spool which contains a length of film and a longer length of " duplex " paper, which is black on the inside and red or green on the outside. The extra length of duplex paper, fitting between the flanges of the spool, protects the film from light, but the arrangement should not be tested too greatly. The spool should be handled with care, never allowing the paper and film to become loose on it, and when out of the camera it should be carefully protected from direct strong light.

There is a cylindrical chamber in the camera to accommodate the spool, where it is held between two spindles, on which it runs freely. Its movement is checked to some extent by a spring. The spool must be placed in the chamber so that when the paper is pulled out and across the picture space the black side of the paper will face towards the lens. Sufficient of the paper is pulled out to reach a second, empty spool, to which the end of the paper is connected by tucking it into a slot in the core of the spool. The camera is then closed and, by means of a key which is fitted to the camera for the purpose, the film is wound forward until " No. 1 " appears in a little red window at the rear of the instrument.

The numbering is printed on the outer side of the duplex paper, and those sizes of film which are intended to be used in more than one type of camera may bear several series of numbers. The photographer need not worry about this, as the correct numbers will come into line with the inspection window in his camera.

It is also customary to print on the duplex paper some warning device, such as a series of dots, or hands, which come into view before the number is reached, and thus avoid the likelihood of the photographer winding the film too far forward.

Whatever the film being used (panchromatic film usually has green and black while colour materials have yellow and black duplex paper) always try to keep the little red window covered except when you actually need to look at the number. Most cameras have a hinged or sliding cover for this purpose to make it easy to comply with this recommendation. Some of the more expensive cameras have automatic numbering devices which make it unnecessary to use the window after you have positioned "No. 1."

Miniature-camera loading is the same in principle, except that the spool is contained in a cassette or patrone, and no duplex paper is used.

Roll-film loading can be carried out in daylight.

Whether a miniature camera or roll-film camera is being loaded the camera-instruction book should be carefully followed. Although the loading of most cameras is similar in principle they differ in detail. It is unwise to assume that because two cameras may at first sight look alike their internal mechanism is necessarily identical. One of the most important rules to observe is always to try to load the camera in the shade, out of direct sunlight. The protective cassette or duplex-paper backing is safe enough if treated sensibly, but if there is the smallest imperfection in the container or in the fitting of the width of the paper between the flanges of the spool upon which it, and the film within its layers, is wound then in bright sunlight some unwanted light may leak in and cause premature exposure of the film to light. This causes what is known as " fogging " of the film: if slight it may only spoil the edges of the film, but if serious it may show up after processing as a grey veiling or as streaks across the picture.

Flat films must be handled in the darkroom. They are loaded into thin metal sheaths, which are thereafter treated as plates. An alternative method is to sandwich the film between a sheet of white glass free from blemish (a cleaned-off plate) and a piece of card and load the sandwich into the plate-holder; but this displaces the film backwards, and allowance has to be made for this when focussing.

Plates are also handled in the darkroom. Fast and panchromatic plates are best handled in complete darkness. You will find that flat films are packed in their box with the sensitive surfaces of all the pieces facing the same way. Plates are generally packed in pairs, with the sensitive surfaces facing inwards. If in doubt, bite the extreme corner of the film or plate, when the sensitive emulsion side will tend to stick to your tooth, BUT DO NOT FINGERMARK the sensitive surface. When card separators are used in the box, they will be placed between the sensitive surfaces of two adjacent plates.

In the single metal plate-holder the plate or flat film is loaded with the sensitive surface facing upwards towards the sliding cover. It is slid or clipped into position and the cover slid over it.

Some cameras have double-plate holders, carrying two plates facing outwards. Sometimes the two plates are placed back to back, with a separator between, and slid or dropped into position in the holder. Generally the holder opens like a book (and is called a book-form dark slide), with a separator sheet hinged between the two halves. The plates or flat films are then placed *face downwards* in position in either half, held by clips, and the whole plate-holder is closed and locked. It is then locked in position on the camera when it is desired to make an exposure.

The plate or flat-film user must cultivate the habit of removing the sliding cover of the plate-holder before making an exposure, *but* do not, in a double slide, remove the wrong cover.

Finders.—You cannot see the actual picture which is falling upon the film, so it is necessary to have some device to show you what the film is " seeing " at the moment when you make the exposure. That device is known as a finder.

The simplest is the *frame finder*. You place your eye at a spot indicated at the back of the camera, and look at the subject. The portion which is surrounded by a wire or sheet-metal frame on the front of the camera constitutes the picture which you are taking. When working very close to the subject, this type of finder does not indicate the picture with absolute accuracy, but it is excellent for most work, and is preferred by many workers. It is extensively used by pressmen. It has the advantage that when taking rapidly moving objects you can see them coming into the " field " of the picture before they actually arrive there, and so make your exposure in good time.

The " brilliant " finder consists of a small lens facing the subject, a piece of mirror behind the

lens which bends the light upwards, and a somewhat larger lens the shape of the picture, in
which the scene is viewed. Two of these finders
are generally built into a box camera, one for
upright and one for flat pictures. On folding
cameras the finder itself can be swivelled to left or
right for the same purpose.

The straight-through optical finder is generally

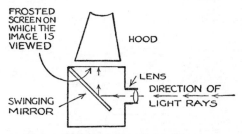

Fig. 3.—The Single-lens Reflex Camera.

in the form of a tube of square section, fitted
solidly to the camera, facing the subject, and with
lenses back and front. This gives a brilliant
image of the subject, and the front lens is sometimes engraved to show the field covered by
different lenses.

The Reflex Camera.—The reflex camera provides
view-finding de luxe, because until the moment
of exposure a mirror at an angle of 45 degrees
intercepts the light from the camera lens and
reflects it upwards to a ground-glass screen at the
top of the camera, where the picture can be viewed
full size (but reversed left to right), and can be

focused accurately (Fig. 3). This device also allows for the exact composition and arrangement of your picture right up to the moment of exposure; then, when the button is pressed, the mirror swings out of the way and the film or plate is exposed.

Another variety of this instrument is the twin-lens reflex, which is essentially a box-camera at

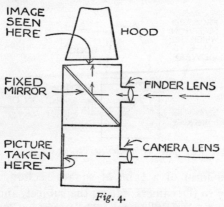

Fig. 4.

The Twin-lens Reflex Camera.
The finder lens is exactly matched to the camera lens.

the bottom, and another similar camera above it which acts only as a view-finder, but is so linked with the bottom one that both " see " the same picture and both are in focus at the same moment. (Fig. 4.)

EYE-LEVEL OR WAIST-LEVEL

Apart from the points mentioned above, the main difference between the direct—frame and straight-through optical—finders, and the in-direct—brilliant and reflex—finders, is the type of view which is obtained. The direct finders enable the camera to see the subject from the eye-level of an ordinary man; the cameras can be swung into position rapidly and operated easily. The reflector-type finders tend to give a chest or tummy viewpoint, while the operation of this type of camera is generally a more leisurely affair.

BUYING YOUR FIRST CAMERA

However much you can afford, buy something simple and inexpensive. The refinements and elaborations which are an advantage to the skilled worker are just an embarrassment to the beginner. Owning elaborate apparatus is not being a photographer, it is the pictures that count. You can do perfectly good work on the cheapest box camera, if you know how. When you *do* know how you will be much more competent to use a more elaborate instrument.

OPERATING THE CAMERA

As soon as you have obtained your new camera, *read the makers' instructions*. They have been written and printed for your benefit. Following the instructions carefully, open the instrument and identify all the internal parts.

Now, *with the camera empty*, go through the motions of taking a photograph. From the very first moment try to adopt the same sequence of movements every time, until the actions become instinctive.

In the case of a simple box camera, the sequence will be : sight the picture through the finder (it may take a little practice to operate the brilliant finder easily) ; operate the shutter lever to make the exposure; wind on the film, checking the number of the next picture in the window provided; always remembering to put back the hinged or sliding cover as soon as you have wound on the film.

With the slightly more elaborate roll-film camera, with ever-set shutter, the procedure will probably be as follows: Make an exposure observation or meter reading and set the diaphragm or stop; focus the camera; sight the subject through the finder; make the exposure; wind on the film.

With an even more elaborate roll-film camera it will additionally be necessary to: set the exposure time on the shutter; wind the shutter mechanism by means of the lever provided; then the camera can be focused and the subsequent operations carried out.

In practically all new cameras, from the simplest box type to the most complex, the mechanisms for winding on the film and for operating the shutter are interconnected so that as soon as the shutter release has been pressed it cannot be used again until the film has been moved on to the next number.   Similarly, the film cannot be wound on again until an exposure has been made on it, so that the user is prevented from taking two exposures on the same part of the film or from leaving it unexposed.   In the more advanced miniature cameras the act of winding on the film also winds up the shutter, whilst focusing is accomplished by means of a range-finder which is coupled to the lens-focusing mechanism.

If you use a plate camera, the sequence will be :—

Exposure reading ; set diaphragm ; set shutter ; focus the camera ; insert plate-holder and withdraw the cover of it ; make exposure, immediately replace the cover of the plate-holder and remove plate-holder from the camera.   If you use a double-sided plate-holder, always place the earliest number towards the lens first, so that the plate or film on that side is exposed before the other, and always indicate unmistakably on the plate-holder when a plate has been exposed.

The actual method of operating the shutter is important.   See further remarks at the end of Chapter III.

CHAPTER II

THE LENS

As has been explained in Chapter I, a pinhole will form an image, but unfortunately it will pass only a very tiny amount of light, and it is impossible to make snapshots with a pinhole camera. If the pinhole is made larger, a lot more of the light-rays from the subject can get

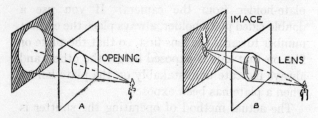

Fig. 5.

A. *The light does not form an image if you enlarge the pinhole.*
B. *The lens bends the light rays inwards to form an image.*

through it, but the picture will be confused and meaningless (Fig. 5 A), because the light spreads out fanwise. If we can bend all these other rays back again so that they hit the film or plate at the same point as the central ray, we shall once more have a recognisable image, but it will be much brighter.

If you put a pencil in a glass of water and look down on it, it appears to bend in the middle, because the water bends the light-rays coming to your eye from below the surface of the water, but does not affect those which come from above the water. Glass possesses the same power of bending light, and if we use a shaped piece of glass called a " lens " (because it is shaped like a lentil), the rays will be controlled in the way we want (5 B).

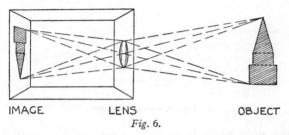

IMAGE   LENS   OBJECT
Fig. 6.

In Fig. 6 we have replaced the pinhole in the camera by a larger hole with a lens in it. It will be seen that a whole fan of light-rays from the top and the bottom of the subject are being collected and directed on to the plate to give a much brighter image. As this applies to every point all over the subject, the whole image thrown on the plate will be brighter, and a snapshot becomes possible.

FOCAL LENGTH

Lenses are identified by their focal length. A roll-film camera may be fitted with what is known as a 3-inch lens, and a large professional camera with a 9-inch lens. Yet, standing side by side, they will both take exactly the same image of the subject, with the exception that the image on the professional camera will be three times as high and wide as that on the roll-film camera.

The focal length is the distance between the film or plate and the lens when the camera is photographing an object which is so distant that

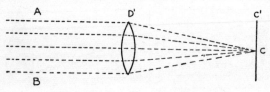

Fig. 7.—Focal Length.

the rays from it may be regarded as parallel (Fig. 7). The lens is then said to be focused at "infinity", which is shown on most focusing scales by the symbol ∞.

In choosing a lens for a camera, consideration is given to the correctness of appearance of the image which will be obtained. If the focal length is too short, the user will tend to work too near to the subject, and, as a result, his foreground objects will be very large, and objects in the background too small in relation to them. If the focal length is very long, he will tend to work from a distance, and foreground and background objects will be too alike in size, and the feeling of depth in the subject will be lost. The happy medium is generally chosen, the rough-and-ready rule being that the focal length of the lens shall be about equal to the diagonal of the picture.

The beginner need not worry about this, as the problem is solved for him by the manufacturer.

APERTURE

The useful area of the lens through which the light is passing is known as the aperture. Two lenses of entirely different focal length photographing in exactly the same conditions will be used at the same aperture, although in fact the actual areas through which light passes will differ very greatly in the two lenses. That is because, although the large lens is letting through more light, that light has to be spread over a much larger area to form a bigger image, and therefore the intensity of light which actually reaches the film or plate in both cases is the same.

Aperture numbers, more commonly known as " f " numbers, show the relationship between the diameter of the hole in the lens and the focal length of the lens. Fig. 8 shows a lens *A B* which gives a focus at *C*, and the size of its opening is indicated at *a b*. The larger circles show that the diameter of the lens opening will go four times into the focal length; the aperture is thus $\frac{1}{4}$ of focus or f/4. The lens would therefore be said to have an aperture of f/4. At *D E*, *d e* we see the result of *stopping down* the opening of the lens to a point where the aperture will go eight times into focal length, and would therefore be f/8 (or one-eighth of f). The "f" number therefore gives the diameter of the aperture as a fraction of the focal length, and, because this is so, the larger the number, the smaller the aperture which is indicated. It will also be realised that the "f" number only refers to the *diameter* of the aperture, whereas the whole *area* of the aperture alters when a lens is opened up or stopped

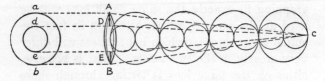

Fig. 8.—Focal Length and Relative Aperture.

down. It will be seen from Fig. 8 that f/8 is only ¼ the area of f/4.

The apertures in a lens are generally controlled by means of an iris diaphragm. This is an ingenious arrangement by means of which a circle at the centre of the lens opens and closes just like the iris of the human eye. The relative apertures to which it can be adjusted are generally indicated on the lens mount, and the iris diaphragm is controlled by means of a ring which revolves round the lens mount.

It is usual to arrange the aperture indications

so that the diaphragm ring is moved anti-clock-wise to open the iris, and clockwise to close it, and so that any indicated aperture is half the size of the one to its left, and twice the size of the one to its right.

A table of these apertures is given below. It will be seen that the continental apertures are slightly different from the English, but for all practical purposes they may be regarded as similar in value :—

Relative areas	1	2	4	8	16	32	64	128
English :								
F. Numbers	32	22	16	11	8	5·6	4	2·8
Continental :								
F. Numbers	36	25	18	12·5	9	6·3	4·5	3·2

The cheap camera, on which the apertures are not marked, generally has an aperture of f/16.

DEPTH

In a pinhole camera the light from the subject is a single narrow ray, so that it does not matter (within limits) where you intercept it with the plate or film. The image will be " sharp " and well defined, and only its size will change.

If, however, you use a lens, you are not dealing with a single ray of light, but with a whole solid cone of rays, and the plate or film must be placed exactly at the point of the cone if the picture is to be sharp. If the point of the cone comes

B—PHOTO

either in front of or behind the plate, the image will be fuzzy.

Some part of the picture must always be fuzzy,

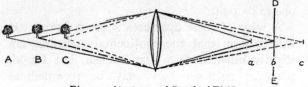

Fig. 9.—Aperture and Depth of Field.

because if, for example, you have three trees at different distances from the camera, the light-rays from them will cross at three different distances behind the lens (see Fig. 9, *abc*).

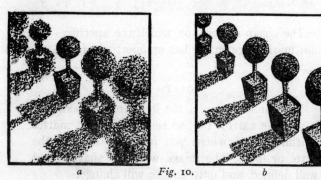

Fig. 10.

(a) *Taken with large aperture.*
(b) *Taken with smaller aperture.*

The smaller the hole, and the nearer therefore we get to single ray, the less pronounced is this effect. The larger the hole the more it is exaggerated. For this reason large-aperture lenses and long-focus lenses (in which the hole is also large) are said to have less depth of field, or " depth ", as it is more generally termed. Depth of field is the distance over which objects at near and far distances can be sharply rendered at one and the same time. In most cheap cameras this depth extends from a point 20 or 30 feet from the camera away to infinity. In the miniature camera the " relative aperture " of the lens can be large—*i.e.*, the lens will be " fast "—but the actual diameter of the opening will be small. It will therefore have considerable depth. This explains some of the popularity of the miniature camera. The beginner in photography is advised to choose a camera which gives a fairly small picture—say $3\frac{1}{4} \times 2\frac{1}{4}$—not only because it will be more convenient to carry and the cost of the material will be low, but also because it will give him some of the advantages associated with the use of short-focus lenses.

ABERRATIONS

While the lens will give a much more brilliant image than is obtained by the pinhole, that image will be subject to distortions or inaccuracies, generally known as aberrations, unless precautions are taken to avoid this.

Instead of the sharply defined images of all the parts of the subject occurring on a flat surface, they may correspond to a saucer-shaped one, in which case the lens is said to have a curved field.

Again, white light contains within it all known colours, and we have all seen the effect of light being split up into these colours by a cut-glass stopper, or some similar object; that is because some colours are bent more readily than others, and a simple lens will therefore create images in the various colours at slightly different distances from it. This is known as chromatic aberration.

With a simple lens, this and other aberrations can be kept to the minimum by working at a small aperture, and for this reason it is possible to fit simple and inexpensive lenses to the cheap forms of camera. As larger apertures are used, the aberrations become more apparent, and the lenses have to become more complex to counteract them. Fortunately, different types of glass bend light in different ways, and so we are in effect able to play one set of faults against another, and thus to balance these inaccuracies.

A lens is an instrument of the very highest degree of precision. The more elaborate ones are difficult to design, and take a considerable time to manufacture, which explains their high cost. It is always safe, from the point of view of correction of aberrations, to use the lens at the largest aperture for which it is made.

THE WIDE-ANGLE LENS

Sometimes it is desirable to fit different lenses to the camera for special work. The photographer may be content to use a small-aperture lens of normal focus for his everyday activities, and may then fit a large-aperture lens for artificial-light work, or when taking high-speed pictures. The more usual changeover is to fit a lens of longer or shorter focus than normal.

The wide-angle lens is of short focal length and, as its name implies, brings the plate or film closer to it, and thus enables it to cover a much wider angle of view than the normal lens.

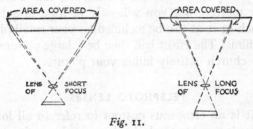

Fig. II.

NOTE.—*The distance between lens and subject and the size of the plate or film are the same in both cases.*

If, for example, you are in a small room, and your ordinary lens will take in only a part of the opposite wall, a wide-angle lens on the same camera will enable you to photograph two, and possibly part of three, sides of the room. Because much more has been crowded on to the plate, the individual items in the picture will be smaller. The images of objects near the edges of the picture will appear distorted because they will reach the plate at a very oblique angle.

THE LONG-FOCUS LENS

On the other hand, it might so happen that you wanted a nice large picture of, shall we say, a church which was on the other side of a river, and your ordinary lens only showed it as a tiny thing in the middle of your picture. You can solve the problem by fitting a longer-focus lens.

A large-sized camera will make a much larger picture of your church. If you take its lens and fit it on your own camera, it will still take a large-size picture, but you will only be able to get as much of it as can be included on your small plate or film. The effect will then be a large picture of the church entirely filling your picture.

TELEPHOTO LENSES

It is an erroneous custom to refer to all long-focus lenses, particularly those used on miniature cameras and amateur cine-cameras, as " telephoto " lenses; this is wrong. A telephoto lens is a special type of objective which can be placed very much closer to the film or plate than the true focal length of the lens. This is accomplished by using a negative lens—*i.e.*, one that is thin in the middle and thick at the edges, which causes the light-rays to diverge instead of converge. The negative-lens system is introduced at the rear of the main lens system. The telephoto method thus enables lenses of quite long focus to be used without the necessity for long extension tubes and other attachments which would weigh down the front of the camera.

LENS HOOD

If you are facing the sun, and the light shines in your eyes, even although not directly in your line of vision, you are more or less dazzled. It is instinctive in such circumstances to shade the eyes with the hand, or to use an eye-shade. An even more efficient device is to look through a short length of tube, which will shield the eye from the rays reflected up from the ground as well as those coming from the sun and the sky. The dazzling effect is due to these rays falling directly on the surface of the eye, and being scattered on to the retina in addition to the light-rays which form the subject at which you are looking. The camera lens is prone to the same trouble. Many cameras, both cheap and expensive, when sold are not equipped with any form of shield which will protect the lens from this effect of light. At the earliest possible moment the photographer should obtain a *lens hood*, which will not only protect the lens from unwanted rays of light, but will also later on prove useful to hold filters which will be referred to in subsequent chapters.

If the lens of the camera is receiving only a very strongly reflected extraneous light such as that from the sky, the effect will be merely to degrade the whole quality of the pictures the photographer takes, causing them to be flat and grey. If, on the other hand, rays of sunlight do strike the lens directly, his negatives will show undesirable rings and bars of light. When working with the camera pointed more or less against the direction of the sun's rays, it is essential that a lens hood should be used.

"BLOOMED" LENSES

It is now customary to coat all glass-to-air surfaces of the components of a lens, and in many cases even the simple lenses of box cameras, with an anti-reflection coating. This additional treatment gives a bluish or purplish tinge to the lens. The coating is extremely thin, durable, and fairly tough, but great care should be exercised in cleaning such surfaces : you will find in most instruction books the maker's recommendations about handling such lenses. . . . Heed their warnings.

A bloomed lens passes a little more light due to the fact that light is not lost in internal reflections, but one of its greatest advantages is that the contrast of the subject tends to be better preserved. However, even with a coated lens it is still wise to use a lens hood in order to take full advantage of such special treatment.

CHAPTER III

THE SHUTTER

EXPOSURE

THE exposure of a film or plate is the combined product of two things :—

1. the *amount* of *LIGHT* which passes through the lens, and is controlled by the *aperture* used, together with

2. the *PERIOD* during which the light passes, known as the *exposure time*.

TIME EXPOSURES

When the lens of the camera is kept uncovered for a period which may vary from several seconds up to several hours in extreme cases, this is referred to as a " time " exposure. Most shutters have a " time " setting (marked T), and with this in operation the shutter control is operated to open the shutter. You can then take the hand right away from the control, and the shutter will only close if you operate the control a second time.

BULB EXPOSURES

These are a brief form of time exposure, generally lasting one or two seconds. A letter " B " on the shutter-mount indicates the setting for bulb exposures. They received this name because one method of giving such exposures is to press and release the bulb which is used to control the shutters of some cameras.

In modern shutters a small lever or special form of flexible release is used, and this is pressed and released. They differ from " time " exposures because the shutter closes as soon as you take your hand off the control.

INSTANTANEOUS EXPOSURES

So-called " instantaneous exposures " vary considerably in length. They are indicated by " I " on the shutter mount. For practical purposes, an instantaneous exposure is made when one pressure of the lever both opens and closes the shutter within a very brief space of time without the need for any further action on the part of the photographer.

SIMPLE CONTROLS

In the earliest cameras, and to-day under certain conditions, long exposures are controlled by removing and replacing a cap on the front of the lens. It is also a practice among professional photographers to hold a thin opaque plate, such as the cover of a dark slide, about ½ inch in front of the lens, to remove the cap, and then to wait for a few seconds until any vibration which may have been caused by this operation has died down. To make the exposure, the metal plate is removed from before the lens, which is left uncovered for the required time; the plate is then returned, after which the cap is again put on. Even the owner of a camera with a modern automatic shutter may find it wise to take advantage of this method of making long exposures, a small piece of card being used instead of the dark slide cover, the shutter being opened in the normal manner before the exposure is actually made with the card, and closed when it is completed.

THE DROP SHUTTER

The earliest effective shutters were those using the principle of gravity. A long strip of thin wood of known weight was carried between two upright rails immediately in front of the lens, and held in an elevated position by means of a small pin or catch. When this pin was removed, the wood dropped downwards at a known speed, and a hole in its centre uncovered the lens for a short period of time. In its simplest form this device would give only one exposure time, and various methods were adopted to obtain variation of the speeds.

BETWEEN-LENS SHUTTERS

Shutters are, in the main, divided into two classes; the first of these is known as the " between-lens shutter ". As the name implies, it works between the elements of the camera lens, and the shutter-housing also forms the mount for the lens. In the simpler forms two blades work scissors fashion to open and close the aperture; but in the more complex forms several blades of carefully designed form are used, calculated so that as little time as possible is lost in the opening and closing of the blades, whatever the duration of the actual exposure. These shutters are generally regarded as being relatively more efficient for " slow instantaneous " exposures than for very short, *i.e.*, " fast " exposures.

The following shutters are of the " between-lens " type, although the " click " shutter is generally used in conjunction with a single lens.

THE CLICK SHUTTER

Fitted close to the lens, this simplest form of shutter, which is still extensively used, consists of a very thin steel blade which is free to rotate about a pivot. A small spring under tension is connected to a release button, and the action is very much like that of an electric-light switch. When the button goes down, the blade flies upwards, and vice versa. There is a hole in the blade which momentarily uncovers the lens as the blade moves up or down, the exposure time being generally about 1/25th second. Sometimes an additional lever is provided which stops the blade in the middle of its stroke, retaining it with the hole opposite the lens until the operator releases it. This gives bulb or time exposure.

EVER-SET SHUTTERS

In the majority of cameras above the really cheap class, the " ever-set " type of shutter is used. It is only necessary to depress the operating lever in order to work the shutter, as it is always set ready for use. Generally it is provided with three settings, marked " T ", " B ", and " I ", respectively, and corresponding to the types of exposure described above. " I " generally gives an exposure time of 1/25th second.

In the more expensive types of " ever-set " shutter " I " is represented by a series of figures marked, for example, 25, 50, and 100, and meaning exposure times of 1/25th, 1/50th, and 1/100th second, respectively. These exposure times are seldom entirely accurate, but they are sufficiently so for all purposes which will be practical with this type of camera and shutter.

PRE-SET SHUTTERS

These are the most highly developed form of the " between-lens " type of shutter. The best of these are extremely delicate instruments of precision, and the standard of accuracy of the exposure time is very high.

The exposure lever does nothing but release the mechanism at the moment of exposure, and the shutter will not work until it has been " set " or wound up by moving a small arm some distance round the shutter mount.

The Compur shutter is generally agreed to be the best of this type, and is fitted on the most expensive models of very many cameras.

It is also extremely popular as a shutter for miniature cameras. Some Compur shutters will give instantaneous speeds as short as 1/500th second, and speeds of 1/300th second are even more common.

DELAYED ACTION

Many shutters of the " between-lens " type are fitted with a " delayed-action " control. When the shutter lever is depressed, the actual exposure is not made until about 10 seconds later. This period varies with different makes of shutter, but in all cases allows sufficient time for the photographer to walk round and get into the picture before the exposure is made.

FOCAL-PLANE SHUTTERS

The second main class of shutter is known as the " focal-plane " type. The focal plane corresponds with the front surface of the plate or film. This type of shutter works as close to that surface as possible. It is simple in principle, but is distinctly superior for high-speed photography with exposures as short as 1/1000th second.

The principle is that of a spring-driven roller blind with a slit across it. Imagine such a blind fitted to a window, but double the usual length, and with a roller at the bottom as well as the top. Only the top roller will be spring-driven, but it will be possible to wind the blind down by hand until half of it is on the bottom roller, and to hold it temporarily in position by means of a catch. Halfway along the length of the material is a slit across its full width, and when the blind is wound on to the bottom roller, the slit is at the bottom of the window. If the catch is released, the blind travels rapidly upwards, and the slit travels the whole height of the window from the bottom to the top. Although it may take 3 or 4 seconds for the slit to travel the entire height of the window, the light will shine into the room through any given part of the window for only a fraction of a second. If an enormous plate or a piece of film were placed inside the window, the effect would be of a bar of light travelling up the plate, each portion of which would be exposed to the light for a fraction of a second.

In cameras, the spring roller is generally at the bottom, and the slit travels from top to bottom in making the exposure. It has given its name to the " focal-plane " cameras used by the press men.

It is also used in the reflex type of camera, as it is possible to synchronise its action more readily with the movable mirror in the camera than would be the case with a " between-lens " shutter, which moves in and out as the camera is focused, while the blind protects the film until the mirror is out of the way.

The more highly developed miniature cameras use the " focal-plane " type of shutter, and in some cases the slit moves from right to left.

Practically all modern " focal-plane " shutters

are " self-capping "—that is, when the blind is being wound up, the two halves of it overlap slightly, so that there is no slit to cause premature exposure, and the slit opens only when the blind is travelling in the correct direction to make an exposure.

Variations in exposure time can be made by :—

(a) varying the tension of the spring which drives the shutter, thus causing it to move faster or slower ;

(b) varying the width of the slit, and

(c) combinations of both of these.

The tendency these days is to keep the tension and therefore the speed of travel of the slit always the same, and merely to alter the width of the slit.

As mentioned above, although the exposure on any part of a plate or film may be very brief indeed, the total time taken by the slit to move over the film is much longer. With very rapidly moving objects this sometimes leads to distortion, and is responsible for the " leaning-forward " effect found on pictures of motor-cycles and motor-cars moving at a high speed. There is little tendency to this fault on miniature cameras, owing to the very short distance which the shutter has to travel.

LOUVRE SHUTTERS

An interesting type of shutter which may be mentioned in passing is the " Louvre shutter ", which was developed in this country for use on aircraft cameras. It has the advantages of being very accurate at extremely high speed, without the distortion associated with the " focal-plane " shutter.

Simply described, it consists of a series of slats which open and close like a Venetian blind placed in front of the lens.

OPERATING THE SHUTTER

The camera must be absolutely still at the moment of exposure. Wrong operation of the shutter control will cause it to move. The smaller the camera the more important is this fact.

Shutter controls consist of (*a*) a lever at the side of the shutter mount, or (*b*) a knob or button which is pressed into the body of the instrument.

NEVER *PUSH* THE SHUTTER CONTROL

If you are working with the camera at waist level and the lever or button has to go downwards, put the thumb on it and the forefinger below the camera, and *squeeze* the two together. Do it slowly—do not jerk.

If the lever has to come upwards, put the finger under it and the thumb on the top of the camera and *squeeze.*

Most eye-level operated cameras have a press button. Adopt the same *squeezing* method, using thumb and forefinger.

If you use a flexible wire (antinous) release, put the thumb on the end of the piston, the first and second fingers behind the flange of the tube, *see that you are not pulling the wire taut,* and squeeze gently.

For time exposures use the wire release, or the card mask method, with the camera on a tripod.

Always have a steady support. If your tripod is whippy and likely to wave in the breeze, weight it down with a heavy stone suspended by means of a piece of string from the tripod head.

Still cameras help to make sharp pictures.

CHAPTER IV

MAKING A NEGATIVE

HOW THE IMAGE IS PRODUCED

WE have seen in Chapter I how a series of light-beams from the subject of varying intensity throw a picture on to the film or plate. The film or plate is coated on its surface with what is known as a " photographic emulsion ", which consists of silver salts suspended in gelatine. It is a peculiarity of these salts that where they have been struck by the light, they can be changed into metallic silver particles by the action of certain chemical fluids, but these fluids have little or no effect on the other parts which have not been light struck. This operation is known as " developing ". The silver particles which make up the picture look black, because they are not present as solid specks, but in the form of tiny spongy or coke-like masses.

The darkness or density at any part of the developed " negative " will depend on the amount of light which has reached that part of the plate or film during exposure. For example, if you photograph somebody in a white dress standing in front of a brick wall in which is an archway with an intensely dark interior, the white dress will cause an intense beam of light to shine on the film where its image is being recorded, and at this point nearly all the silver salts will be reduced to silver. The beams from the brick wall will be much less intense, and only a portion of the emulsion will be reduced to silver during development. Probably no beams of light will reach the film from the archway interior, and consequently little or no silver will be formed during the operation of development.

As the residue of silver salts will not be required after development, it is dissolved away by means of sodium thiosulphate, generally known as " hypo ", this operation being called " fixing ".

If the image is now examined, it will be seen that the intensely light dress has created an intensely dark image, and the dark interior of the arch has left a light and transparent image.

In other words, the values of the image will be in negative relationship to the tones in the original subject, hence the practice of calling this first record a " negative ".

TYPES OF SENSITIVE MATERIAL

Negative material is obtainable in two main forms : either as glass plates, or as film.

Glass Plates have the disadvantages of weight and susceptibility to damage by fracture, but they are used for many purposes, because they possess the outstanding advantages of absolute flatness, and the absence of any tendency to expand or become distorted during the various operations of developing, fixing, and washing.

Film is light in weight, and it is obtainable in very compact packings. There are developing and printing houses all over the country which are equipped to deal with film rather than with plates.

The amateur will be most familiar with the *Roll Film*, of which many millions of spools are used each year, the most popular being that known as " 20 " or " 120 " size. Almost as popular is 35 mm. material, the name deriving from its width, which has perforations along each edge facilitating the transport of the film through the camera.

With the increasing use of colour materials picture sizes have tended to become smaller because most processes produce transparencies for projection rather than prints for viewing in the hand. Whereas a few years ago 8 pictures $3\frac{1}{4}'' \times 2\frac{1}{4}''$ on 120 roll-film was the rule, the tendency now is to arrange for 12 pictures $2\frac{1}{4}''$ square on the same length of material. In addition to the well-established picture size of $1\frac{1}{2}'' \times 1''$ on 35 mm. film, others of $1''$ square and $1'' \times \frac{3}{4}''$ are not unusual, while an even smaller one on 16 mm. width material is coming into favour.

Flat Film is also available to the plate-camera owner. It is a very much thicker material, each piece of which is generally placed in a thin metal sheath, the film and sheath then being loaded into the ordinary plate dark slide.

COLOUR SENSITIVITY

When we look at a subject we see it in full colours, but the photographic material we use only records it as a series of greys.   Light colours as well as light tones are reproduced as pale greys. Rich colours are shown as darker greys.

But the film or plate does not " see " the colour in the same order of brightness as the human eye.   For example, we think of golden hair as being very bright.   Some kinds of film would show it as very dark grey.   Again, red lips are also brilliant to the eye, but would come out black to some kinds of film.

On the other hand, quite a dark blue sky will come out white on some films and plates, because they respond so readily to blue light.

The more sensitive a plate or film is to a particular colour, the lighter the tone of grey in which it appears in the photograph.

The earliest plates were " blind " to practically all colours of light except blue.   Luckily a lot of blue light is reflected back from the surfaces of objects of all colours, and consequently this defect is not so serious as it might have been ; but things like red bricks, yellow hair and green grass looked very wrong in early photographs.

Very little of this type of film or plate is now sold for ordinary photography, and does not concern us here.   Nearly all films and plates in these days may be divided into three classes :

" Normal   Panchromatic "—sometimes   the
brand name may contain the termination
" chrome " which used to be associated with
a type of emulsion known as " orthochromatic" which was not sensitive to orange and red.

" Fast Panchromatic "—two or three times as
sensitive to light as the normal speed materials.

" Super-speed Panchromatic "—about twice as
fast again as the " fast " types of material, enabling photographs to be taken under very
poor lighting conditions: this kind of photography is usually referred to as " available
light photography ".

Panchromatic materials, as the designation
implies, are sensitive to all of the colours in the
spectrum. Of the various types available, those
in the normal and fast categories will reproduce
appropriately in terms of black, grey and white,
the range of colours in a scene. On the other hand,
the super-speed materials tend to be over-sensitive
to orange and red and to reproduce these colours
rather lighter than they should.

Panchromatic film of normal speed should be
used for out-of-doors photography, where accuracy
of tone rendering is aimed at. It can also be used
for the copying of pictures, tapestries, the photography of flowers, and similar subjects needing
accurate interpretation, and it is suitable for
artificial-light work, since most sources of artificial
light give out a large proportion of red rays.

Super-panchromatic film is specially designed to

be used in artificial light for high-speed photography, or in order to obtain exposures where the minimum of artificial light is present—*e.g.*, night photography in the streets. It is not entirely suitable for daylight out-of-doors photography, because of its exaggerated response to red. For example, in the case of a portrait, it is very likely to render the lips much too pale.

COLOUR FILM

A large number of makes of colour film are available for use by professional and amateur. These are divided into two main categories: one known as *reversal*, which produces transparencies for projection from the film used in the camera, and the other *negative-positive*. See Chapter XI.

FILTERS

At this point it is appropriate to make a brief reference to the use of filters in black-and-white photography.

In the tail-lamp of a car is a white light, but because there is a red glass over it, anybody looking at the lamp only sees red light. The red glass is a filter which has soaked up all the other colours in the white light, and only allowed the red rays to pass on.

Photographic filters are pieces of coloured glass or gelatine, which are placed in front of the lens of the camera, the object being to hold back a proportion of the rays of light of certain colours, and thus prevent those colours from receiving **too** much exposure in relation to the other colours.

For example, a yellow filter will definitely retard the passage of blue light, whilst freely passing yellow and red light. In taking a landscape, this would have the effect of causing the blue sky to appear darker, thus throwing into greater relief any fleecy clouds which might be present, and preventing the sky from dominating the whole picture by presenting too large an expanse of unrelieved light tone. For out-of-doors work it is usual to use a pale yellow filter with orthochromatic film. A green filter with panchromatic film will fulfil the same purpose.

It will be realised that if some of the light is held back in this way, it will be necessary either to increase the aperture or the time of exposure, to ensure that the same total amount of light will reach the film. The film will receive the same amount of exposure, but the proportions between the different colours will have been altered. The amount by which the exposure has to be increased is known as the multiplication factor of the filter.

FILM AND PLATE SPEEDS

Some photographic material is more sensitive to light than others. The highly sensitive material is said to be " fast," and the less sensitive material is said to be " slow." If comparative exposures are made under exactly the same conditions, using the same aperture and exposure time, the faster film negative will have upon it a much heavier silver deposit than the slow material, and will be said to be " denser ".

An over-exposed negative will be too dense, and an under-exposed negative will be too thin. A perfect negative should contain a reasonably accurate rendering of all the desired tones in the subject. This will be dealt with at greater length in Chapter VII.

SPEED FIGURES

To know what exposure is correct under a given set of conditions, it is necessary to know the " speed " of the film, and to enable this to be done, speed figures are issued for the various materials. Of these systems of speed notation " H. & D." is the oldest. Those now used include A.S.A., B.S.I., D.I.N., Scheiner and Weston. The figures are arrived at by different methods, and there is no true comparison between them, although it is the practice to issue tables of comparisons. Any discrepancies in these tables are more than allowed for by the " latitude " of the material, which is briefly a quality of the film or plate which enables the theoretically correct exposure to be departed from to some extent, without noticeable degradation of the results obtained.

ESTIMATING EXPOSURE

The correct exposure is one which enables an image to be recorded on the film which most truly represents in tones of grey the scale of brightness of the original.

Correct exposure can either be estimated, or arrived at by means of an exposure meter. A number of the film manufacturers, and the publishers of many periodicals and technical books, issue charts which enable exposures to be calculated. These charts generally allow for : (a) different times of the day; (b) different times of the year; (c) different states of the light and weather conditions; (d) different types of subject.

For example, a photograph made in the middle of the day, in the middle of the year, under bright-light conditions, of a fairly distant subject, would require merely a fraction of the exposure time as compared with a photograph of a subject taken early or late in the year, early or late in the day, under dull light, of a subject close to the camera. A characteristic table is printed below, by kind permission of the Editor of the *Amateur Photographer*, the well-known photographic weekly. The *A.P.*, as it is generally called, prints such a guide in booklet form and also in the *Amateur Photographer Diary*.

There are mechanical exposure calculators embodying these principles.

EXPOSURE METERS

Exposure meters can generally be divided into three groups :—

(a) The Extinction type of meter, in which the user observes the subject through a piece

The exposure table is based on British Standard No. 935 (1957) and can be implicitly relied upon for accuracy, Adjustments are indicated for summer time.

USING THE TABLES

The use of these tables is simple. First check to see whether your camera has an exposure value scale (sometimes erroneously called a light value scale) marked on the shutter. If it has, take one number (printed in a heavier type) from each table, from I to IV, add the numbers obtained together and read off the exposure value in Table V. For cameras without the exposure value scale, use Tables I to IV, then Table VI and the exposure will be found opposite your total in Table VII.

Example. Suppose an unshaded nearby subject is to be photographed on Ilford F.P.3 film on a lightly overcast day in June at 5.30 p.m. (British Summer Time), without using a filter. Reading the numbers corresponding to these conditions from Table I onwards they are 10, 1, 4, and 4: total 19. From Table V we find that this is equal to an exposure value of 19. If your shutter is not marked with an exposure value scale you will need to take account of the stop to be used (see Table VI). If using f/8, for instance, the total would now be 27, and Table VII indicates a exposure of $\frac{1}{50}$ second. This may not be marked on your shutter, but the nearest, $\frac{1}{25}$, will be near enough.

Filters. Add an extra figure when using a filter (this is *not* the filter factor).

| Filter factor | . | 1½ | 2 | 3 | 4 | 6 | 8 | 12 | 16 |
| Figure to add | . | 1 | 2 | 3 | 4 | 5 | 6 | 7 | 8 |

Notes. If experience shows that negatives consistently turn out denser than required, subtract 2 or more from total before using Table V or VII. When it is difficult to decide between alternative conditions, for instance whether a subject is lightly (6) or heavily (8) shaded; split the difference and take the figure 7.

TABLE I

In the following Table films are arranged in groups of approximately similar speed values for use with the Exposure Tables.

Black-and-white Films

Factor 0

Agfa: Record · · · Kodak: Royal-X Pan

Factor 4

Ilford: H.P.S.

Factor 6

Adox: R.25, KB.25	Hauff: Pancola S.25
Agfa: Isopan Ultra	Ilford: H.P.3
Gevaert: Gevapan 36	Kodak: Tri-X
Guilleminot: Guilpan	Perutz: Peromnia 25
Reportage	Zeiss Ikon: Contapan 25

Factor 8

Adox: KB.21, R.23, 21	Ilford: Selochrome Pan
Agfa: Isopan ISS	Kodak: Verichrome Pan,
Coronet: Corochrome	Plus X
and Pan	Lumiere: Altipan
Ferrania: Pancro 32	Mimosa: Panchroma 21
Gevaert: Gevapan 33	Perutz: Peromnia 21
Hauff: Pancola S.23, 21	Standard: Ortho and Pan

Factor 10

Adox: KB.17, R.17	Hauff: Pancola 17 and
Agfa: Isopan 17 or F	18
Crumiere: Aviapan	Ilford: F.P.3
Ferrania: Pancro 28,	Lumiere: Altipan 17
Ultracromatico 30	Mimosa: Panchroma 17
Gevaert: Gevapan and	Perutz: Perpantic 18
Gevachrome 30	Zeiss Ikon: Contapan 17

Factor 12

Adox: KB.14, R.14	Ilford: Pan F
Agfa: Isopan FF	Kodak: Panatomic X
Gevaert: Gevapan 27,	Perutz: Pergrano 14,
Dia-Direct	Reversal
Hauff: Granex 14	

Colour Films—Roll and Miniature

Factor 7

Kodak: High Speed Ektachrome

Factor 8

Ansco: Super Anscochrome

Factor 10

Adox: C.18 · Agfa: CT.18 · Perutz: C.18

Factor 11

Adox: NC.17	Ferrania: Ferrania negative
Agfa: CN.17	Gevaert: Gevacolor R.5
	Ilford: Ilfacolor

Factor 12

Gevacolor: N.5	Kodak: Kodachrome II
Ilford: Ilfochrome	

Factor 13

Agfa: NC.14	Ferrania: Ferraniacolor
	reversal

Note. Some of the above films are not available in Britain.

Month	11–1	10–11 1–2	9–10 2–3	8–9 3–4	7–8 4–5	6–7 5–6	5–6 6–7	4–5 7–8	a.m. p.m.
June	0	0	0	0	1	1	2	3_6	June
May	0	0	0	0	1	1	3	5_9	July
April	0	0	0	1	1	2	3_6	—	Aug.
Mar.	0	1	1	1	2	3_6	—	—	Sep.
Feb.	0	1	1	2	3_6	—	—	—	Oct.
Jan.	1	2	2	3_4	—	—	—	—	Nov.
Dec.	1	2	3	4_7	—	—	—	—	Dec.

In Tables II and IIa the last heavy figure in each line refers to the end nearest midday of the period shown; the small figure is an estimated value for half-way through the period. These are calculated for the middle of each month, and must be used with caution at the beginning or end.

Mth	12–2 2–3	11–12 3–4	10–11 4–5	9–10 5–6	8–9 6–7	7–8 7–8	6–7 8–9	5–6 —	a.m. p.m.
June	0	0	0	0	1	1	2	3_6	June
May	0	0	0	0	1	1	3	5_9	July
Apr.	0	0	0	1	1	2	3_6	—	Aug.
Mar.	0	1	1	1	2	3_6	—	—	Sep.
Feb.	1	1	1	2	3_6	—	—	—	Oct.
Jan.	1	2	2	3_4	—	—	—	—	Nov.
Dec.	1	2	3	4_7	—	—	—	—	Dec.

1–3 3–4	12–1 4–5	11–12 5–6	10–11 6–7	9–10 7–8	8–9 8–9	7–8 9–10	6–7 9–10	a.m. p.m.

Times at the head of Table IIa refer to Summer Time, those at the foot to Double Summer Time.

TABLE III.   *Light.*

Clear sun	.	.	.	.	.	0
Hazy sun	.	.	.	.	.	2
Cloudy, bright	.	.	.	.	.	4
Cloudy, dull	.	.	.	.	.	6 or more

TABLE IV   *Subjects.*

Clouds, open sea	.	.	.	.	0
Distant and Semi-distant	.	.	.	2
Nearby, unshaded	.	.	.	.	4
Nearby, lightly shaded	.	.	.	6
Nearby, heavily shaded	.	.	.	8
Close-up, unshaded	.	.	.	.	6
Close-up, lightly shaded	.	.	.	8
Close-up, heavily shaded	.	.	.	10

For side-lighting in sunlit scenes, add 1.
For back lighting in sunlit scenes, add 2.

Total	Exp. Value	Total	Exp. Value	Total	Exp. Value
37	2	25	8	13	14
35	3	23	9	11	15
33	4	21	10	9	16
31	5	19	11	7	17
29	6	17	12	5	18
27	7	15	13	3	19

TABLE VI.   *Stops.*

f/2	0	f/3·5	3	f/5·6	6	f/11	10
f/2·5	1	f/4	4	f/6·3	7	f/16	12
f/2·8	2	f/4·5	5	f/8	8	f/22	14

For box cameras, take stop-factor as 11.

TABLE VII.   *Exposure.*

No.	Exp.	No.	Exp.	No.	Exp.
16	$\frac{1}{1250}$	27	$\frac{1}{30}$	38	$1\frac{1}{2}$
17	$\frac{1}{1000}$	28	$\frac{1}{20}$	39	2
18	$\frac{1}{700}$	29	$\frac{1}{15}$	40	3
19	$\frac{1}{500}$	30	$\frac{1}{10}$	41	4
20	$\frac{1}{350}$	31	$\frac{1}{8}$	42	6
21	$\frac{1}{250}$	32	$\frac{1}{6}$	43	8
22	$\frac{1}{150}$	33	$\frac{1}{5}$	44	12
23	$\frac{1}{100}$	34	$\frac{1}{4}$	45	16
24	$\frac{1}{75}$	35	$\frac{1}{3}$	46	24
25	$\frac{1}{50}$	36	$\frac{1}{2}$	47	32
26	$\frac{1}{40}$	37	1	48	48

COMPARATIVE FILM SPEEDS

Exact conversion of film speed ratings from one system to another is impossible because of the different principles employed in each method. The table below should only be regarded as an approximate guide for exposure-meter purposes.

B.S. (degrees)	A.S.A. Weston	D.I.N. (degrees)	Weston (Old)	Factor (Table I)
20	8	10	6	16
23	16	13	12	14
26	32	16	24	12
27	40	17	32	11
28	50	18	40	11
29	64	19	50	10
30	80	20	64	9
31	100	21	80	9
32	125	22	100	8
33	160	23	125	7
34	200	24	160	7
35	250	25	200	6
38	500	28	400	4
41	1000	31	800	2
44	2000	34	1600	0

Scheiner speeds are one unit higher than the B.S. Speed Index; American G.E. figures are $12\frac{1}{2}$ per cent. higher than the A.S.A. Speed Index.

of transparent material containing a number of tones in progressive stages of greyness, which may be numbered or coded. By observing either the last number which it is possible to read clearly, or the behaviour of the details of the subject seen through the scale of tones, it is possible to choose the exposure which can be calculated on scales supplied with the meter. This is a very rapid means of ascertaining exposure, and a number of these devices are quite cheap, but they cannot entirely take into account the variation of the sensitivity of the eye under different lighting conditions.

(b) The Photo-Electric Meter. This type of meter incorporates a light-sensitive cell which generates electricity when light falls upon it. The needle of a micro-ammeter in the circuit moves over a calibrated scale, from which indication, by means of other scales or tables, the exposure may be arrived at. Photo-electric meters may be divided into two sub-types : (i) *reflected* light meters, and (ii) *incident* or " high-light " meters. The former measures the light reflected from the subject, while the latter is used to measure the light falling on the subject. Some meters may be converted from reflected to incident types by means of adaptors. Quite a number of roll-film and miniature cameras have built-in exposure-meters for greater convenience.

(*c*) The Photometer type of meter, in which the brightness of the filament of a small lamp or a spot within the field of view is compared with the brightness of a selected part or parts of the subject or field of view. An excellent example of this kind of meter is the " S.E.I. Photometer " marketed by the Ilford organisation.

The photographer is strongly urged to use some form of exposure meter. While the value of the film he saves may not, for some time, amount to the cost of the meter, he will be saved the chagrin of losing important and irreplaceable pictures due to his own inaccurate estimation of exposure. This is much more important than the saving of a few shillings or pounds. The newcomer to photography will find that with the aid of an exposure meter he can learn very much more rapidly to be an expert operator, than if he gropes in the dark unaided.

At the same time I would issue a warning against becoming utterly dependent on the exposure meter, or taking its readings without modification to suit the circumstances. The exposure meter is merely a scientific instrument for measuring quantities of light which are present. According to the type, it will tell the photographer (*a*) the total amount of light being reflected from *all parts* of the subject or (*b*) the intensity of the light falling upon the subject. The actual exposure to be given will vary slightly according to the distance of the subject, the nature of it, whether a more faithful rendering is required of the dark or light portions of it, and the manner in which the exposure reading has been taken. The photographer must be aware of all these factors. Reference to the " *A.P.*" exposure chart will give an indication of the allowances which have to be made for different types of subject under the same conditions of light. It will be seen from this that a meter reading taken on a landscape, for example, would not indicate with any degree of accuracy the exposure required for a portrait. The correct way to take a reading for a portrait is to approach closely to it with the meter, so that the angle covered by the meter includes the subject to be photographed, *and nothing else*.

If the subject is mixed in character, some allowance will have to be made. For example, a group of men in grey suits against a softly lit background might give the same reading as a bride in her white dress in front of a dark church porch. In the former case the exposure indicated by the meter can be used. In the latter case about half the indicated exposure would need to be given, or the bride's frock would be over-exposed, because it is much lighter than an average of all the tones in the picture. If the background were also light, the meter would automatically indicate a smaller exposure.

CHAPTER V

THE DARK-ROOM

A COMMON FALLACY

IF the film or plate is examined after exposure, no sign of the image can be seen, but it is lying concealed within the sensitive material and at this stage is known as the " latent " image. To make it apparent, it must be treated in suitable chemical solutions, and this work must be carried out in a dark-room.

Because of its name, a large number of people are under the mistaken impression that the dark-room should be a gloomy place painted black, or as near black as is possible. This is entirely wrong.

The best colour for a dark-room is white or cream, or some similar light tone, as this form of decoration will make the most use of the illumination within the room. It is a dark-room only in the sense that it is not lit with ordinary white light, but with light of a colour to which the film, plate, or later on the paper which is being used in it is not sensitive, or only very slightly sensitive.

THE DARK-ROOM LIGHT

Except for panchromatic materials, most others are blind to red light, and a " safe-light " of this colour can be used to illuminate the dark-room when handling non-colour, sensitive materials, such as bromide and chloro-bromide papers. Panchromatic material is sensitive to all colours, and therefore no coloured light is really " safe " to use with it. It so happens, however, that while human vision is particularly sensitive to green light, panchromatic plates are less so, and it is therefore possible to use a very dark green safe light with this material. The material can, however, be exposed to it for only very limited periods, and must not be brought close to the light.

Very slow materials, such as lantern-slide plates and bromide printing-paper (which will be referred to again in Chapter VIII), can be handled in a yellow or light-brown safe light. What is known as gas-light paper can be handled in ordinary-room light, providing that this is not too intense and that the direct rays from the light-source do not reach the paper until completion of the operations involved.

THE POSITION OF THE SAFE LIGHT

Another bad habit which is practised by many photographers is to have the light-source comparatively near to, and shining down upon, the work space, with the result that the films or plates are in a dangerous position near the light, while most of the room is in funereal gloom. It is better to place your light high up, so that a larger part of the room is illuminated, while the best plan is to use a more brilliant source, and arrange it so that it points upwards, allowing only the ceiling and the walls to receive the direct rays, which are then reflected down on to the working space. In this way a much greater amount of general illumination can be used, the

Fig. 12.—Distribution of Light in Dark-room with Reflected Light Scheme.

room will be freer from cast shadows which might hinder the worker, and at the same time the material is safe from being accidentally light-struck (Fig. 12).

"SAFE" LIGHTS

It will not suffice to use any type of coloured light, as all red light, for example, is not " safe ".

You can obtain from your photographic dealer suitable " safe lights " either in the form

of a coloured fabric, dyed gelatine sandwiched
between glass with or without diffusion material,
or glass shields which totally enclose the electric
bulb. An electric bulb of not more than 15
watts should be used for direct light, while complete lamps suitable for various types of light
source can also be obtained.

THE IDEAL DARK-ROOM

The ideal dark-room should contain a long,
narrow work-bench about waist high, leading at

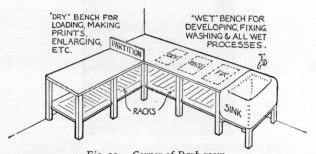

Fig. 13.—Corner of Dark-room.
The marked squares indicate the position of dishes when in use.   Racks under
are for storing dishes, etc.

one end to a square porcelain sink fitted with a
plug and cold-water tap, preferably of the bottle-
filling type, which has a very narrow nozzle
giving a thin stream of water which does not tend
to splash. Shelves or racks below the bench
can hold the dishes, measures, and other equipment (Fig. 13). A cheap wooden cupboard can
be used to contain stocks of plates and paper,

but these should be kept low down, lest they become contaminated by rising fumes or gases. The best plan is to keep them outside the dark-room in a similarly low position. An electric kettle is a convenience, but should be as far away as possible from the sink. A gas-ring can be used instead, but if there is no ventilation, the stored plates and paper may suffer.

The window should be rendered opaque in some suitable way. This can be done by a shutter of three-ply wood or blanketing or canvas material, heavily painted on both sides and stretched on a frame held in the opening by turn-buttons. The edges of the shutter should be fitted with rubber draught-stopper tubing or strips of felt, so that when it is pressed tightly into the window-frame there is no leakage of light. Particular care should be taken to eliminate such leakage, as with modern fast films and plates trouble may arise from " fogging ".

The door of the room can, with advantage, have similar draught-stopper run round the two sides and the top, while an inexpensive draught-excluder of the rising type should be fitted at the bottom. The effectiveness of these measures can be tested by staying in the room in absolute darkness for about five minutes before making observations.

VENTILATION

The above arrangement does not allow for ventilation, and if a very small room is being used it will rapidly become unpleasant to work in. Ventilation can be provided by cutting into the plywood shutter, and, if the landlord does not mind, the door also, a 9-inch-square hole which is fitted with a " light trap " as shown in Fig. 14. The interior of such a trap should be painted with flat black paint.

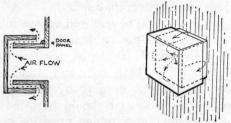

Fig. 14.—Ventilation Light-trap.

MAKING THE BEST OF IT

Most workers will not be able to obtain such ideal conditions. A good substitute is the family bathroom. A five-ply top can be prepared, about half the length of the bath and of the same width, with two rather deep battens which will stiffen the plywood top and fit just across the interior of the bath to prevent the top moving (Fig. 15), and raising it enough to avoid having to stoop. The same precautions as previously described will be necessary to prevent white light entering the window and door.

Some photographers will be forced to work in the cupboard under the stairs. In cases where the entrance to this cupboard is a door of normal height below the stairs, this may not be inconvenient, but it will be wise to scrape away all loose paint or whitewash, and thoroughly clean and redecorate the interior with washable distemper. If the underside of the wooden stairs can be seen, it will be wise to panel it with sheets of thin ply, as otherwise dirt may work through

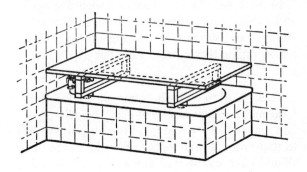

Fig. 15.—Ply Cover for Bath with Deep Battens.

and cause trouble. Ventilation through the door panel will be essential. While a sink and running water are a convenience in the workroom, they are not absolutely necessary. An enamel pail full of water will provide for rinsing and immediate requirements, and the domestic sink can be used for final washing.

ESSENTIAL EQUIPMENT

In addition to a suitable dark-room light, the following equipment will be necessary :—

    (1) A thermometer.
    (2) Suitable dishes or containers.
    (3) Measures for fluids.
    (4) Dark-room clock.

THERMOMETER

This is for testing the temperatures of solutions, which must be strictly adhered to if exact work is to be done. Do not buy one with fine figures and a thin mercury column : the indications must be bold to be read in the dark-room. Proper photographic thermometers are not expensive.

DISHES

These are to contain films or plates during treatment. They can be of glass, bakelite, porcelain, enamelled steel of good quality, or xylonite, in that order of preference. For plates, the dishes should have an internal dimension at least 1 inch larger than the plates, and should preferably have lines and hollows moulded in the base to make it easy to pick up the plates from the bottom of the dish.

For flat films, similar dishes can be used, or the films can be treated in tanks specially designed for the purpose. These tanks are comparatively expensive.

Roll films, provided they are not too long, can be developed by the " see-saw " method, in which the film is held at its extremities by the two hands. One end is then placed in the solution and drawn through it and out at the other side. The other hand follows with the rest of the film. The operation is then reversed, and continued by moving the hands up and down, " see-saw " fashion, with the loop of film between them, keeping the bottom of the loop always in the fluid. This can be done in a deep dish, but requires a certain amount of skill. A better container for this purpose is a good-quality pudding basin of small size, as its use reduces the likelihood of the film being scratched. Only one end of the film need be held and raised and lowered out of and into the solution, allowing the other end to uncoil and coil under the surface of the solution.

Fig. 16—The Johnson " Universal " Developing Tank.

Long lengths of film and miniature camera film should be treated in special tanks which hold the material in spiral form so that the whole of it can be immersed in the solution. There are a number of different types of tank, and full instructions are given with each when sold (Fig. 16).

KEEP DISHES SEPARATE

Where dishes or basins are used, at least three will be required : one for developing, one for rinsing, and one for " fixing ". The fixing-dish or basin should be clearly marked, and should never be used for any other purpose. The final washing after fixing can be carried out as described in Chapter VI.

When developing tanks are used, all of the processing operations can be carried out in them, including the final washing, when a stream from a tap is directed into them.

MEASURES

Whether the user buys his developers in ready-mixed powder form, or in prepared solutions, or mixes them himself, he will require fluid measures to enable him to pour out exact quantities of various fluids. One 10-oz. or 20-oz. measure and one 1-ounce measure will be sufficient to start with. These should be first-quality chemical measures, but a 30-oz. glass jug obtainable from the cheap stores will also be convenient for handling larger quantities of solution.

Mixing of one's own solutions will necessitate a pair of scales. Proper photographic scales, or good-quality letter scales, or a letter balance can be used. It is suggested that from the very beginning the photographer should adopt the metric system of weighing and measuring chemicals and fluids, as this is more precise and simple than the avoirdupois method, and is increasingly favoured by most photographers.

DARK-ROOM CLOCK

Correct time of development is as important as correct temperature of the solutions, and a clock should be used to control this. Suitable photographic clocks can be obtained which will measure seconds and minutes and can be returned to zero at will. Some are fitted with an alarm, and some have luminous hands. The main essential is that they should have easily-read faces, the preference being for black letters on a white ground. A cheap alarm clock can be used, but it is far better to afford the proper article.

ADDITIONAL ACCESSORIES

The above are essentials, but the following accessories are also desirable :—

(1) Clips for roll film, flat film, and film-pack exposures, to avoid finger marking and similar damage to the films.

(2) Washing-tank for plates.

(3) Viscose-sponge or wash-leather for wiping off excess moisture after washing.

(4) Drying-rack for plates.

Later on the photographer may acquire print forceps of bakelite or stainless steel for handling prints and enlargements in the developer, and a print-paddle for handling them in the fixing-bath.

This avoids the danger of contamination of one solution with another by the wet fingers.

Another desirable accessory is a drying-cupboard, which can be a tall, narrow, whitewood cupboard of the cheapest kind. A hole about a foot square can be cut in the bottom, and another out of the door near the top, and covered in each case with thin muslin. This will allow a free

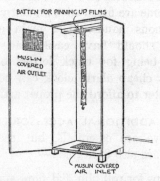

Fig. 17.—A Drying Cupboard.

passage of air and ensure that the film or plates are drying in a dust-free atmosphere (Fig. 17).

PREPARATION OF SOLUTIONS

Whenever possible, solutions should be made up with boiled water. If this is not possible, and the water is known to have lime in it, trouble may be avoided by adding a small quantity of Johnson's Calgon to the water before starting to prepare the solution. The maker's instructions as to mixing solutions should always be followed very carefully, and in the absence of special instructions, the chemicals should be dissolved in the order given in the formula, making sure that each chemical is completely dissolved before adding the next. The only exception to this rule is that it is desirable to dissolve a pinch of the preservative before adding the other ingredients, as this avoids oxidisation. A developer consists of :—

The Developing Agent, such as metol, hydroquinone, amidol, pyrogallic acid.

Accelerating Agents, which cause the developing agent to work, such as potassium carbonate, sodium carbonate, caustic potash, caustic soda, borax (used in fine-grain developers).

Preservatives, which resist the tendency of the developer to combine with oxygen and become stale, such as sodium sulphite, potassium metabisulphite.

Restrainers, such as potassium bromide and ammonium bromide. These act as a brake on the developing solution, and avoid the production of flat grey images.

KEEPING CHEMICALS

Buy crystals and powders of good quality from a photographic dealer or a chemist who specialises in photographic goods. These will generally be supplied in appropriate containers, and in some cases the bottles will be coloured, because the chemicals are susceptible to light. Some chemicals are deliquescent—that is, they tend to take up moisture from the air. Others are efflorescent, and rapidly give up the water in them. It is not necessary to remember the differences between all these chemicals, provided they are all kept well sealed and in a dark place. Solutions obtained ready made should be kept in accordance with the maker's instructions, but should always

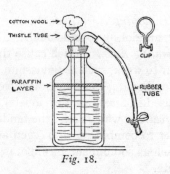

Fig. 18.

be well stoppered. When preparing your own solutions, it is generally possible to make these up in a concentrated form which can be used as stock solutions, and a proportion taken and diluted with the required quantity of water at the time of use. It is better to keep a large quantity of a stock solution in several small bottles which are quite full, than in one large container. The small bottles should be well corked, and the corks sealed by means of melted candle wax. In this way the contents are protected from the air.

If solutions are kept in large bottles, they are exposed to a fresh supply of oxygen every time the stopper is removed, and become stale; but if it is more convenient to use a large bottle, a good plan is that indicated in Fig. 18. The bottle is replenished from time to time through the thistle tube, which can conveniently be stopped with a wad of cotton wool. The solution is drawn off through the other tube, which forms a siphon. It is even better if a bottle can be obtained with a tap at the bottom. Immediately after the bottle is first filled, and before the bung is thrust home, a quantity of medicinal or toilet paraffin is carefully poured in to form a layer about $\frac{1}{4}$ inch deep, which acts as a permanent floating lid on top of the solution.

KEEPING WORKING SOLUTIONS

Use stoppered bottles which hold exactly the quantity of working solutions and no more. Always filter solutions when returning them to the bottle.

Do not keep used developer solutions if it can be avoided. A developer that has been contaminated by use deteriorates much more rapidly than an unused one. If, therefore, some time is likely to elapse before you will need it again, it is better to throw it away.

A good plan, when developing one film or plate, is to use just sufficient solution for the job, and then discard it. This is another advantage of the

small pudding-basin for roll films : it requires
less solution than a flat, open dish.

If you *must* use developers several times, discard them as soon as, in daylight, they show
marked discoloration. If solutions are used more
than once, allowance must be made for deterioration by prolonging development time.

Plain hypo solutions should be discarded after
use.

Acid-hardening fixing-baths keep fairly well,
but should be discarded as soon as the fixing
action starts to slow down. Another indication
of staleness of the fixing-bath is frothing when it
is poured back into the bottle.

CHAPTER VI

DEVELOPING THE NEGATIVE

STAGES OF DEVELOPMENT

WHAT is loosely referred to as " developing " a
film or plate really consists of several stages :—

   (a) the actual development ;
   (b) intermediate washing, or rinsing ;
   (c) fixing ;
   (d) final washing ;

and if desired—

   (e) final hardening, or " anti-scratch " bath ;
   (f) rinsing after above solution to remove
        excess hardener, prior to drying ;
   (g) drying.

All these operations must be carried out with
care if first-class results are to be obtained.

TEMPERATURE

It is of the utmost importance that solutions
should be at the correct temperature, and that
as near as possible all solutions should be of the
same temperature, including (and this is often
overlooked) the rinsing water between the baths.
If photographic material is placed into a warm
solution, and then into a cold one, and back
again into a warm one, and so on, the gelatine

will probably become distorted and wrinkled—a trouble known as " reticulation ". There are a number of ways in which solutions can be warmed in cold weather and cooled in warm weather. Hot or cold water must not, of course, be added to the solutions, as their strength will thereby be altered; but the bottle containing the solution can be placed in a saucepan of water to raise temperature, or held under a running tap or placed in a pan with ice to lower it.

The best plan of all is to keep the dark-room itself as near as possible to the ideal temperature of 68° Fahrenheit (20° Centigrade), and keep the various chemicals in this temperature for some hours before use. The rinsing water can easily be brought up to this temperature, and if the day is really cold, the film or plates càn be allowed to cool down before final washing.

MAINTAINING TEMPERATURE

If it is impossible to keep the room at the correct temperature, it will not be sufficient merely to bring the solutions to the right one if work is to be carried on for some little time. For instance, on a cold day the coldness of the air and of the plates and films will rapidly cool off the developing solution. This can be avoided to some extent by placing the dish of developer inside a larger dish containing warm water. Another method is to make a shallow box, with holes cut in, which will take the dishes, and to burn a carbon filament or similar electric lamp inside the box. It must, of course, be light-tight.

On extremely hot days the developing dish may be surrounded with cold water or ice, although that precaution will seldom be needed in this country.

DEVELOPMENT TIME

The lower the temperature, the longer the development time, while at about 55° Fahrenheit (13° Centigrade) some chemicals become completely ineffective. Above 75° Fahrenheit (24° Centigrade) there is some danger that the gelatine on the film, plate or paper will become unduly soft, and in some cases may dissolve, particularly when long and complicated operations involving a number of solutions are carried out.

Different types of material require different development times. Generally speaking, the faster films and plates require longer development than slower films and plates. It will be seen that both the material and the temperature can affect the correct developing time, which may vary as widely as between five minutes and twenty minutes with the same solution. The manufacturers of developers and the producers of developing formulae give correct developing times for their solutions, or this information can be obtained from the inquiry departments of the excellent photographic magazines which are published in this country.

DEVELOPMENT METHODS

There are three recognised methods of development :—

(1) *Development by Inspection*—consists of watching the negative until the image on the back attains a density which experience shows to be the correct one. It is practically impossible to do this with panchromatic film, as even if a dark green safe light is used, there is not enough light to make judgment certain.

(2) *The Factorial Method*—consists of watching for the first appearance of the image, multiplying this time by a given figure or " factor ", and carrying on the development for this length of time. Again it is difficult to carry out this method with panchromatic film, and there are theoretical objections to it, although it has some strong adherents.

(3) *Time and Temperature*—consists of placing the film in the developer, and retaining it there for the correct time appropriate to the temperature given on the manufacturer's chart, irrespective of the amount of exposure which it has received. Most films are developed in this way, and it is in theory the most correct method. It is earnestly recommended to the beginner in photography, because it will remove one element of uncertainty from his early work, and thus enable him to see quite soon the direction in which his

exposures tend if they should not happen to
be correct.

PREPARATION

If yours is a makeshift dark-room, start by
putting out *all* the lights, and then, by waiting for
a brief while, ensure that no unwanted exterior
light is leaking in.

Then arrange your developing equipment.
Place the dark-room clock where it can be easily
seen and controlled.

If you are developing in open dishes or bowls,
place them on the bench in the order (*a*) developer,
(*b*) rinsing bath of water, (*c*) fixing bath, (*d*)
washing tank, which can conveniently be placed
as near as possible to the dark-room sink. It is
better not to place it *in* the sink, in case some
sudden need should arise to use the latter.

If you are developing by spiral tank, you will
only need the tank for the actual solutions. For
rinsing and washing, a small rubber tube should
be provided. A small-diameter tube can be stuck
inside the bore of the wash-basin tap and inside
the entrance hole to the tank. If you have a
bottle-filling tap, this will not be necessary.
You should also provide, in addition, a funnel
and some pure cotton wool. A small pad of cotton
wool placed in the funnel will act as a filter when
returning solutions to their bottles. If you
use a glass funnel of 5-inch diameter you will be
able to empty the solution from the tank into the

funnel as fast as it is capable of emerging from the pouring opening, without overflowing the funnel.

Similar filtering should always be carried out when returning solutions to their bottles.

When setting out your developing equipment, always arrange it in exactly the same place and the same order; you will then be able to find it without difficulty in complete darkness.

Now check the temperatures of your various solutions and, if necessary, bring them to the correct one. This should be checked again at intervals while you are working.

You are now ready to turn on the dark-room light and turn out the white light.

Having done this, unpack the exposure to be developed. Before doing so remember—DO NOT TOUCH A FILM OR PLATE ON ITS SENSITIVE SURFACE. You will find it quite easy to handle it by its edges. The sensitive side is nearly always the dull side—the only exception being plates which have been backed with certain substances of non-reflecting character.

A roll film will have the seal on it which you stuck down after exposing it. Incidentally, when sealing a film you should turn in the end before sticking down the paper seal. You will find that it is then easy to slit the seal with the thumbnail when you wish to unroll the film.

Pull out the paper, and you will come to the loose end of the film. Fasten a clip to it, and then gently pull out the rest of the film from the roll, detaching the other end from the backing paper.

If you are going to develop see-saw fashion, put a clip on the other end. If you use a pudding-basin, only one clip need be used.

If you use a spiral tank, set the spider frames in the tank to the correct width and gently load the film into the spiral until the whole of it has been taken up. HOLD THE FILM BY ITS EDGES. The dull side is the sensitive side.

Flat film will be removed from the plate-holder first in its metal sheath, and then from the metal sheath.

Glass plates will similarly be removed from the plate-holders. Remember that the sensitive side of the emulsion will face (*a*) upwards towards the covering slide of a single plate-holder, (*b*) outwards in the case of a double-holder. This means, in the case of a book-form slide, that when the two halves are hinged apart, the plates present their backs towards the photographer. Backed plates will be rougher on their backed side than on the sensitive side.

All materials should be placed in dishes with the sensitive surface facing upwards, or away from any surface with which the film or plate may make contact.

SEQUENCE OF OPERATIONS

Some workers advocate first wetting the film or plate with water to ensure that no bubbles are formed when it is put into the solution. This is not necessary with modern materials, as a surface-tension reducer is incorporated with them which ensures that the solution flows evenly over the surface.

PLATES

The solution can be poured rapidly over the plate from a measure, or the dish can be tilted to the left, and the plate slid in quickly from the right, while the dish is brought back to a flat position, thus causing a wave of developer to flow over the plate. If a tank is used, the plate should be held by the outer edges of the two top corners between the thumb and forefinger of the right hand, and slid down into the solution in one smooth movement, then withdrawn and lowered again, to avoid the possibility of air bells.

Flat-film and single-pack exposures can be slid quickly under the surface of the developer in a dish, or inserted into a tank in correctly designed frames or " hangers ".

ROLL FILM

The operation of "see-saw" development has been described. If a spiral tank is used, the film is loaded into the spiral, which is put in the tank and the lid put on. Solution is poured smoothly and rapidly down the central tube in the lid in one continuous operation. Any slight difference between the time of immersion of the bottom of the film and the top does not matter, because diluted developers are used in tanks, and the period of development is relatively long.

AGITATION

It is most important to agitate the dish or tank during development. If this is not done, the waste products of development will flow down the surface of a vertical plate of film, or lie stagnant on the surface of a horizontal plate or film, causing incomplete and uneven action. Dishes should be rocked continuously in an irregular or uneven manner, tanks at frequent intervals. Water-tight tanks can be inverted from time to time. Spiral tanks are provided with a rod which is inserted at the top and permits the spiral to be revolved. It should be turned anti-clockwise, otherwise, in most tanks, the film will come out of the spiral. It is advisable to give the spiral half a dozen turns to the left, then to stop it abruptly, then give a few more turns, and so on, otherwise the solution may revolve in the tank at the same rate as the spiral, and there will be little effect of agitation.

RINSING

On completion of development the film and the solution should be separated as rapidly as possible, and the film briefly but thoroughly rinsed. This avoids contamination of the fixing solution with stale developer and development products, which might have an adverse effect on the film and interfere with the action of the fixing-bath.

FIXING

The film or plate will still contain the balance of the sensitive emulsion which has not been acted upon by light and developed into a negative. This must be "fixed"—*i.e.* dissolved away. The chemical which is universally used for this purpose is sodium thiosulphate, otherwise known as "hypo". This chemical has a double action, first turning the unwanted salts into another compound, and then dissolving this away. When the film or plate is immersed in this solution, the milky appearance disappears and the rough-and-ready rule is to retain the film in the solution for twice the time that it takes to become clear. With a stale hypo bath the film may not be properly fixed, although it appears to be quite clear, and the photographer should have no hesitation in throwing away the solution if there is any doubt as to its fresh and active nature.

At this point the importance of fresh solutions of all kinds cannot be too much emphasised. Many photographs are spoiled by the mistaken attempt on the part of their makers to save developers, fixing and other solutions, by using them as long as possible. The cost of these chemicals is low as compared with the cost of the photographic material, and, if the user takes his hobby seriously, the production of good results is much more important than the saving of a few odd pennies.

ACID-HARDENING FIXING-BATH

Hypo is rarely used alone. The simple solution will soon be contaminated by carried-over developer, and will turn brown, staining negatives and prints. To avoid this, sodium sulphite or potassium metabisulphite is used as preservative. It is also usual, with fixing-baths used for negative material, to add a hardening agent, such as alum or chrome alum, to protect the film from undue swelling or blistering, and to give it added resistance to subsequent wear.

SEPARATE HARDENING BATH

In some cases this hardening is carried out separately in an alum bath. Sometimes a mixture of alum and formalin is used. If this is done, the film should be washed for about twenty minutes between fixing and hardening.

FINAL WASHING

After fixing, the hypo must be removed entirely by means of washing. Perfect washing is not necessarily obtained by the violent use of large quantities of water. It is necessary for the water to be changed, in order to take away the hypo removed from the photographic material, but the elimination of the chemical is due to its diffusion from the supporting gelatine into the water. This action cannot be hurried beyond a certain point, however rapidly the water is circulating.

PLATES

A single *plate* can be washed in a flat dish by tilting it slightly and allowing water to flow in gently at one corner and out at the other. It must not drop directly on the surface, or blistering will occur.

A number of pieces of *flat-film* can be treated in a similar way, provided that they are held apart with suitable clips or in developing hangers. Larger quantities of *plates* or *flat-films* must be washed in a suitable tank, with an outlet near the bottom; that is because hypo-laden water is heavier than ordinary water, and however violent the flow, would remain untouched at the bottom of an ordinary tank. Most tanks of this type have a syphon through which the water emerges. Syphon attachments can be obtained to hang over the sides of deep dishes to ensure removal of the flow from the bottom of the dish.

Roll films which have been processed by hand offer a little more difficulty. Such a film can be placed in a loose coil in a large basin which is gently filled with clean water and left standing for five minutes. It is then entirely emptied, rinsed out, and again filled with water. This operation should be carried out five or six times at intervals of five minutes. If the two ends of the coil are held together with a wire paper-clip, it is less likely to become damaged, but do not put the clip on any part of the film which contains a picture. Another plan is to pin the film by its two ends to a long piece of wood, and float it on the top of a bath half full of water. It can be left for an hour, and the hypo will diffuse from it and drop to the bottom of the bath. Films developed in spiral tanks are washed by allowing the water from a tap to pour into the hole in the centre of the lid.

Widely varying times have been given as the correct period of washing by running water. These have varied from sixty minutes down to as little as ten. In my experience, thirty minutes in running water, or six changes at five-minute intervals, is adequate in most cases, providing the operation has been thoroughly carried out in properly designed equipment. Incomplete washing will result in the eventual deterioration of the image.

DRYING

Correct drying is also important. A dust-free drying-place of even temperature should be chosen, and once drying has commenced, nothing should be done to interfere with its rate of progress by altering the position of the negative.

Plates should be dried on a proper rack, and should be spaced as far apart as possible. The glass side should be wiped free from water and, if the plates have been hardened, the emulsion side can also be wiped gently. If this is not done, the drops which collect at the lower corner of the plate should be removed with a piece of wadding from time to time, without removing the plate from the rack.

Separate pieces of *flat-film* can be pinned up by one corner in a position where they hang free and spaced apart from one another. Excess moisture can be removed from them gently, which operation is facilitated if developing-frames have been used. In this case they can be dried in the frames.

Roll film or 35-mm. film can be dried by attaching a clip at each end and hanging the film vertical in a suitable place. Provided the films have been hardened, they can be wiped down on both sides, bearing in mind the fact that the back as well as the front of most roll films is covered with gelatine. The back of 35-mm. film is plain celluloid.

WIPERS

It is essential that the materials used to wipe plates or films are delicate and free from grit and dirt.

First-quality cotton wool which has been wetted and squeezed nearly dry is sometimes used for plates, but is the least effective of the three things mentioned here.

First-quality wash-leather will remove a con-

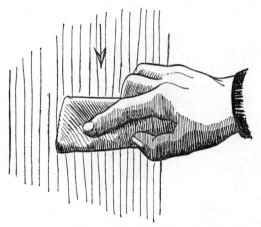

Fig. 19—Wiping with Damp Wash-Leather.

siderable proportion of the moisture.   When first obtained it should be thoroughly washed and wrung until all foreign matter and dressing are removed, and should afterwards always be kept in a covered tank of water.   For wiping a negative, it is wrung as dry as possible, folded, and used as indicated in Fig. 19.

Viscose sponge is the best material of all.   It is a by-product of artificial silk.   When dry it is comparatively hard, but it will take up very considerable quantities of water, and when wet is soft and delicate. It can be used as a sponge in the ordinary way on plates, flat-films, and film-pack exposures, but for wiping film it is advisable to slit it down the middle and use it as shown in

Fig. 20.—Wiping with Viscose Sponge.

Fig. 20. This has the additional advantage of protecting the working surface from unwanted dirt.

PROTECTING THE NEGATIVE

As soon as the negative is dry it should be placed in a protective envelope, to avoid accumulation of dust and scratches. The smaller the negative the more important is this advice.

Soft paper gives a
very flat result with
a normal negative,
but would make an
excellent print from
a contrasty negative.

Normal contrast
paper is suitable for
a normal contrast
negative, bringing
out all the details
and the full range
of tones.

A flat, overexposed
negative or one
which had been
under-developed
would be printed
on very contrasty
paper. With a
normal negative the
result is much too
harsh.

The same subject considerably over-exposed, having received eight times the exposure of the previous negative. Although it appears darker and flatter the detail is all present and a first class print could be obtained from this negative.

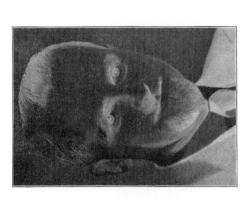

A correctly exposed negative. At no point is this negative entirely transparent, while detail may be found in all but the very darkest shadows.

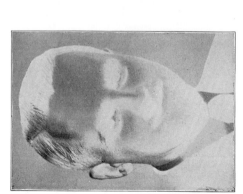

An under-exposed negative. Notice the complete absence of detail in the light portions, which represent the shadows of the subject.

CHAPTER VII

NEGATIVE CHARACTERISTICS

EXPOSURE AND DENSITY

THE density or darkness of any part of a negative depends on the exposure. When there has been little exposure—*e.g.*, from the shadow portions of the subject—the negative will be thin and transparent. Where there has been plenty

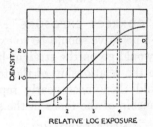

Fig. 21.—Curve showing Speed and Character of Film or Plate.

of exposure—*e.g.*, from light and bright portions of the subject—the negatives will be definitely dense and opaque.

THE CHARACTERISTIC CURVE

The characteristics of a particular film can be indicated by drawing a curve which indicates the increases of density consequent upon known increases in exposure. Such a curve is shown in Fig. 21. In this the increases in exposure are read from left to right along the base line, while the increase in density is indicated by the height above the base line. It will be seen that the curve is roughly S shaped, and that while the increase in density from B to C is quite regular in relation to the increase in exposure, the curve is much flatter (that is, increases in density are much less) on the sections A–B and C–D for a given increase in exposure. The section A–B is known as the " toe " or under-exposed portion of the curve; section C–D is the " shoulder " or over-exposed portion of the curve.

CORRECT EXPOSURE

In theory, a negative should be so exposed that its densities would go on the straight-line portion B–C, because the relationship of the tones in the negative would then most nearly represent the actual relationship of the tones in the subject.

UNDER-EXPOSURE

In practical fact a considerable amount of work is done on the " toe " or under-exposed portion of the curve of the emulsion, particularly by amateurs with cheap cameras, and professionals doing high-speed and artificial-light photography. Such under-exposed negatives will not only be thin, but also " flat "—that is, low in contrast— and a print from such a negative would normally be dull and dark. It is, however, possible to overcome this disadvantage to some extent by suitable choice of printing paper, as will be explained in Chapter VIII.

OVER-EXPOSURE

A negative which is made principally on the portion $C-D$ of the curve would be over-exposed and very dense and opaque. There would be a tendency towards flatness, but less so than in the case of under-exposure. It would give a light, washed-out print, which would also lack contrast.

THE SAFER ERROR

While theoretically correct exposure is always best when making your negative, it is much better if an error is to be made that this should be an error of over-exposure rather than under-exposure. Under-exposure gives you a negative from which some of the essential information is missing, and this cannot be added by subsequent chemical treatment. Over-exposure will give a very dense negative, but the information will have been recorded in it, and if necessary it will be possible to secure a print from it either by longer printing, more intense printing light, or chemical reduction of the negative.

EFFECT OF DEVELOPMENT ON QUALITY

The effect of development is to alter CONTRAST. If the negative is developed in a cold solution or for too short a time (*i.e.*, UNDER-DEVELOPED) the negative will lack contrast. As development extends, the various parts of the negative build up density at different rates, the darker parts gaining density more rapidly than the lighter ones. At normal development time the contrast will be correct. A negative developed in a solution which is too warm or for too long a time (*i.e.*, OVER-DEVELOPED) will be too contrasty. (Excessive over-development or too warm solution may also cause veiling or fogging, but does not alter the rule.)

THE TWO RULES

The two rules to bear in mind, therefore, are :—

EXPOSURE CONTROLS DENSITY.
DEVELOPMENT CONTROLS CONTRAST.

NEGATIVE APPEARANCE

There are many photographers of long standing who do not know what a good negative really looks like. The roll-film snapshotter consistently produces grey, ghost-like negatives from which the developing-and-printing houses perform the almost miraculous feat of turning out passable prints, but a good negative will always produce the best results.

A correctly exposed negative should contain neither absolutely clear glass or celluloid, nor absolutely black densities. The thin portions should reveal a slight greyness and some detail if the negative is laid down on to a sheet of white paper, while the dense portions corresponding to the high lights of the subject should just permit good black print to be legible through them if they are laid in contact with the printed material. The range of tones between should be smooth, and not harsh. It is difficult to describe the perfect negative in words, and on Plate 2 has been printed a reproduction of a good normal negative. Even allowing for the necessary loss in reproduction, it should give the worker a basis of comparison.

FAULTS IN NEGATIVES

It is possible that a certain proportion of your negatives will be imperfect, at any rate in the early stages, and the faults may arise from a variety of causes. Some of these are given below :—

Too thin, but contrast almost normal : under-exposed.

Too thin, and also lacking in contrast : probably normally exposed, but under-developed.

Too dense, but contrast almost normal : over-exposed.

Too dense, but very hard contrast : normally exposed, but over-developed.

About normal density but very hard contrast, details lacking in shadows : under-exposed and development prolonged.

About normal density, but the whole picture flat and lacking in contrast, the darkest portions rather thin : over-exposed, but development curtailed.

Normal density but the whole negative veiled over with greyness : fogged.

This may be either by light fogging due to accidental exposure to white light, or to the use of an unsafe dark-room light. If the latter is suspected, place a piece of unexposed material on the work-bench with a small opaque subject, such as a coin or a key, in the centre of it. Leave it there for two minutes, and then develop in absolute darkness. If the light is unsafe, a silhouette of the subject will be observed on the film or plate. If the portion of the negative around the edge which should be covered by the mask in the camera is clear, fogging has most likely occurred while the material was in the camera.

Fogging may also be *chemical*. If material has been kept too long, it may have deteriorated, and this type of fogging is generally shown by extra darkness at the edges of the material.

It may also be caused by unduly warm developer, or too much alkali, or insufficient potassium bromide in the solution. It is often possible to remove fogging by reduction (see p. 105).

Streaks, stripes, and patches of fogging are probably caused by a leaking camera or dark slide, or perhaps by getting the film light-struck during loading or unloading. Such fogging sometimes occurs when roll films are too loosely wound by the user, and light creeps down the edges.

Pinholes and white spots.—These may be caused by tiny dust particles on the film or plate at the moment of exposure. Larger, clear spots, circular or irregular in shape, are caused by air bubbles, grease or oil in the developer, or scum on the developer adhering to the negative.

Transparent finger-prints are caused by touching the surface of the film before development, the natural oil in the skin preventing the developer reaching the exposed image.

Some parts of the negative darker than others, the boundaries being somewhat sharply defined and curved in shape : developer unevenly flowed over the plate when commencing development.

A similar form of marking, but less well defined and somewhat more curved in shape is caused by uneven drying. This can be improved by re-soaking and re-drying the negative.

Black tree-shaped markings, " *Static* ": caused by tiny electrical charges in the film.

Partial reversal of the negative, which in places appears almost like a normal picture : exposure to unsafe light during development. A rare cause is excessive over-exposure, several hundred times normal exposure.

Frilling and blistering : developer too warm, too much alkali, or large differences between the temperatures of successive solutions.

Milky appearance : the negative is not properly fixed, and should be returned to the fixing-bath.

Yellow discoloration : the above defect appears after the negative has been kept for some time before it is observed. Nothing can then be done about it.

White crystalline deposit : this may be hypo crystals due to insufficient washing, or a deposit from excess lime in the local water. First try thorough washing; if not successful, try treatment with 2% solution of hydrochloric acid. Wash afterwards.

Small black spots : possibly caused by minute holes in the dark slide. More likely to be caused by undissolved particles of developer in solutions which are used too soon after mixing.

Honeycomb or mottled appearance : badly mixed or too-dilute developer, or insufficient agitation. Old film.

Image sharp but high lights blurred and sometimes a ring of density surrounding small points of light. This seldom occurs on film, and generally only on unbacked plates. It is known as *halation*, and is due to reflection of light from the glass back of the plate. Backed plates should be used to avoid this trouble.

Blurred soft image : camera is out of focus.

Blurred image with all the details distorted in one direction : the camera was moved at the moment of exposure.

AFTER TREATMENT

If a negative is too thin, it can be improved by intensification, always bearing in mind that the chemicals cannot add details which do not exist, and can only increase existing densities. If a negative is too dense, it can be improved by re-

duction. Farmer's Reducer (potassium ferri-
cyanide and hypo) will tend to increase contrast
while reducing, the effect being greater with a
stronger solution. Fogging may sometimes be
removed by treatment with Farmer's Reducer.
Ammonium persulphate will reduce more evenly.
Wash thoroughly after reducing.

STORAGE

As soon as possible after drying, the negative
should be protected by being placed in a suitable
container, whether it is to be printed from immediately or not. Crystal paper envelopes are
suitable for glass plate, flat-film and film-pack
negatives, and single roll-film exposures. For
the miniature camera film 35 mm. wide, long
sheaths of crystal paper are available which will
take a six-exposure strip. Even greater care is
necessary to protect 35-mm. film from injury than
is given to ordinary negatives, because this type
of negative is generally greatly enlarged. Small
surface defects, dust particles, and other blemishes
which are not noticeable with small degrees of
enlargement become extremely so when the
original picture is enlarged a considerable number
of diameters.

CHAPTER VIII

MAKING PRINTS

THE operation of making a print is chemically the repetition of the making of a negative, inasmuch as the action of light causes the sensitive photographic paper to become developable wherever it strikes the photographic emulsion upon it.

Photographic paper, lantern-plates, and similar material intended for the preparation of the final image are very much slower than negative material. They are not colour sensitive, or at any rate only slightly so in some cases. Such material is generally known as " positive " material, because in the final photograph the picture is dark where the original was dark and light where the original was light. Shadows and high lights take their true values, and, in other words, the tones are in positive relationship with the subject.

TYPES OF PAPER

Printing papers may be divided into the following main classes :—

Fast Materials.—Bromide and chloro-bromide papers, although much slower than negative materials, are still quite sensitive to light and must, therefore, be handled only in an appropriate safe light, usually one of orange or light red.

Slow Materials.—Contact, or gas-light, papers are much slower even than bromide or chloro-bromide papers and can be handled relatively safely in subdued artificial light without the need of a safe-light.

However, unused material should *not* be left exposed to light and the packet or box should be kept closed when not in use.

Bromide Paper.—Like negative material, Bromide paper receives a relatively short exposure which gives no visible image, and the paper has to be developed. Metol Hydroquinone (M.Q.) and Amidol Developers are usually preferred for Bromide paper. An acid fixing-bath should be used, and washing must be very thorough as chemicals cling tenaciously to the fibres of the paper. The image is black or blue-black in colour. This type of paper has a single coating of emulsion only—by putting on two coatings, one of which has a greater contrast than the other, and making each sensitive to a different colour of light, a special degree of control is obtained. Contrast is varied by changing the printing-light.

Chloro-Bromide Papers are of the same nature as bromide, but rather slower and, because of the mixture of silver salts used in their composition, give warm brown tones by controlling the development.

Gas-light Papers.—As has been indicated previously, gas-light paper is one of the slowest of all normal photographic materials, and can consequently be worked in a room lit by ordinary light, provided this does not directly reach the paper. Exposure is relatively short, and development and fixing are necessary, M.Q. or amidol being used. An acid fixing-bath is preferable, and thorough but rapid rinsing between development and fixing is most important.

PAPER CONTRAST

Papers are available with a wide range of contrasts—that is to say, that from the same negative they will give differently contrasted results. Plate 1 shows prints from a normal negative on soft, normal, and contrasty bromide paper, respectively. This range of choice will enable you to adjust to some extent inaccuracies present in your negatives and to secure the results you require. Contrasty papers, particularly contrasty gas-light paper, are used for printing from very under-exposed thin negatives, and contrasty gas-light paper will often give results where all other methods fail.

PAPER SURFACES

You will be able to obtain a great variety of results by choosing the surfaces of the paper which you use. These surfaces include glossy, egg-shell, semi-matt, linen-grained, mechanically mottled, rough and very rough textures. The rougher textures are used rather for big enlargements than for small-size contact prints, and are particularly suitable for enlargements from miniature camera negatives. The glossy surfaces are used for the majority of amateur snapshot prints, and also in cases where the original photograph is intended to be reproduced by a magazine or newspaper. That is because a perfectly polished surface only reflects light in one direction, and the photograph can be lit on the copy board so that there is no unwanted reflection to interfere with the true tones of the photograph when it is copied by the block-maker.

OTHER METHODS

As you become more advanced in your technique, you will be able to experiment with other interesting methods, such as the Bromoil process, which gives a final image composed of oil colour, and the Carbro process, which gives a final image formed of coloured carbon pigment. Both these processes have distinctive appearances and strong adherents in the world of pictorial photography.

MAKING AND FINISHING A PRINT

The operations of making and finishing prints on different types of paper are generally similar, requiring a series of clearly-defined steps or stages, which broadly resemble those of the negative process. The same care and attention is needed throughout the processing, especially with regard to handling and avoiding fingering the emulsion surface.

Although most papers are treated in the same kind of way there may be slight differences in the manufacturer's recommendations—keep to the golden rule and follow the maker's advice.

Many bromide papers can be developed in the same kind of developer, often referred to as a " universal paper developer ".

On Bromide, Chloro-bromide or Gaslight Papers.

(a) Printing with suitable, controlled, artificial light.

(b) Developing.

(c) Rinsing in plain water.

(d) Fixing.

(e) Final washing.

(f) Drying (and in the case of glossy prints these may also be glazed).

MATERIALS FOR PRINTING AND FINISHING
Essential requirements are :—

(a) a printing-frame or printing-box ;

(b) dishes in which to develop and fix the prints ;

(c) a washing device.

THE PRINTING-FRAME
The printing-frame is like a picture-frame with a glass front and a loose back hinged in the middle, and the two halves of the back held separately in contact with the glass by long, flat springs which press on the back. When printing from film negatives the plain glass is left in position, but can be removed with advantage when printing from glass negatives. If the frame is laid face downwards on the work-bench, the negatives should be placed in it with the dull emulsion side facing

upwards towards the worker. The paper is placed face downwards on the negative, and the back placed in position and locked.

The frame should be left lying face downwards until the exposure is to be made, otherwise there may be an additional and uncalculated length of exposure time which will upset the final result.

THE PRINTING LIGHT

If gas-light or bromide paper is being printed, the frame should be supported so that the printing

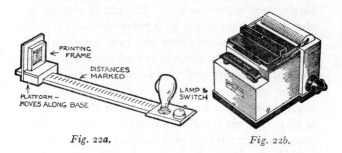

Fig. 22a.   *Fig. 22b.*

light is exactly opposite its centre, and at an appropriate distance from it. The most suitable light is a 25-watt pearl electric bulb. An incandescent gas mantle can also be used. The packets of paper issued by the various manufacturers will contain suggestions for appropriate distances and powers of light, but as an indication a suitable distance with bromide paper using a 25-watt pearl lamp would be about 4 feet, the exposure time being between 1 and 8 seconds.

An opal bulb will give a slightly longer time. With gas-light paper using a pearl lamp at a distance of only 9 inches, the exposure time will be between 10 and 20 seconds.

It is important always to place the frame at *exactly* the same distance from the light, as this profoundly affects exposure. A simple stand can be made as in Fig. 22*a* on p. 111.

PRINTING BOXES

Self-contained printing boxes can be obtained which have an electric light permanently fixed inside them at the bottom. The top of the box is similar in construction to a printing-frame which is facing downwards into the box, except that, instead of the back being in two pieces, it takes the form of a pressure-pad, and is hinged to the frame at the edge farthest from the operator. The nearer edge has a handle, and when the negative is laid down on the glass surface, a piece of paper placed on this, and the pressure-pad brought down, it holds negative and paper in contact and switches on the exposing light as long as the pressure-pad is held down. Some boxes have a red light in them which burns continuously, and allows the negative and paper to be adjusted in relation to one another before the exposure is made (Fig. 22*b*).

DISHES

Dishes should preferably be fairly large in size and always of adequate depth. It is quite safe to have two or three prints lying in the same solution at the same time. They will not damage one another, as they have an "anti-stress" coating which avoids the possibility of marking due to one print rubbing over another. Of course some care must be exercised when the prints are wet, as the gelatine is softened. If you are making $3\frac{1}{2} \times 2\frac{1}{2}$-inch prints, a useful size of dish is half-plate—*i.e.*, $6\frac{1}{2} \times 4\frac{3}{4}$ inches. For half-plate prints a whole-plate ($8\frac{1}{2} \times 6\frac{1}{2}$ inches) dish should be used, and so on. Three dishes will be required : (1) for the developer, (2) for rinsing, and (3) for fixing. They may be of the same materials as are recommended for negative work. Really large dishes are somewhat expensive, but suitable enamel dishes for rinsing may be obtained from any domestic stores. If, however, a dish becomes chipped and rusty, it should be discarded at once.

WASHING DEVICES

Rotary tank washers for prints may be obtained, but are expensive, and are not really necessary for the private worker. It is, however, essential that the washing arrangements should ensure that the prints do not hang together in one soggy, sluggish mass during the operation, as washing will then be quite incomplete. The wash-basin in the bathroom is particularly suitable because of its rounded form, but the tap should be temporarily fitted with a short rubber tube terminating in a narrow nozzle, which can lie near the bottom of the basin. This will give a powerful thin stream of water, which will cause it to swirl round the basin and keep the prints in continuous movement. Larger prints may be washed in flat dishes.

ADDITIONAL ACCESSORIES

If possible the photographer should spend a few shillings in buying a pair of print forceps and a print paddle, the first being used in the developer, and the second in the fixing-solution.

DEVELOPING

Holding the print in a nearly horizontal position at the right-hand edge of the dish, insert the left end in the solution and immediately slide it under the surface of the solution in one continuous movement, so that the whole surface is covered as nearly as possible at the same moment. Rock slowly but regularly, watching for the appearance of the image.

If bromide paper has been correctly exposed, development should be complete in one-and-a-half to two minutes at 65 degrees Fahrenheit. The quality of the print depends on correct exposure and development for the correct time. Over-exposure and short development produce flat, muddy prints. Under-exposure and longer development produce harsh, contrasty prints. If a developer is stale, too weak, or has too much potassium bromide in it, it will give greenish-black results which are unpleasant. Insufficient potassium bromide will give a grey image with veiled whites.

Gas-light paper will develop in about thirty seconds at 65 degrees Fahrenheit. With a properly exposed print, the density will reach a certain point, and then development will slow down considerably, and the image appear not to gain in density. The print should be removed from the bath as soon as possible after completion of normal development, to avoid the onset of fogging. Correct exposure is of importance in securing gas-light paper results of first quality.

When judging prints in the dark-room it should be remembered that the finished print will not appear so dark and contrasty when it is dry and viewed in daylight as it does when wet and viewed in yellow light.

RINSING

The print should be removed from the developer, preferably with print forceps, and moved about in a large dish of clean water. This water should be changed very frequently if a long sequence of work is being done. Rinsing is very important with gas-light paper.

FIXING

Remove the prints from the rinsing water, place them *face downwards* in the dish containing hypo, and immediately press them below the surface with a print paddle, a glass rod, or a piece of clean wood kept for this purpose (and washed thoroughly when finished with). Move the prints about to avoid trouble from air bubbles trapped underneath them, otherwise you may have spot trouble. *Do not put your fingers in the fixing-bath.* Rinsing will not entirely remove the hypo from them. You are then liable to cause discoloration and spots when handling the printing-paper, and also possible contamination of the developer.

If you are doing a large number of prints, do not allow the hypo dish to become full of a mass of prints. It is a good plan to have a second dish of hypo, transferring prints to it after a few minutes' immersion in the first one. As the second dish becomes full, the prints can in turn be transferred to a large bowl of water or to the washing container. Each print should fix for at least fifteen minutes.

WASHING

Washing can be performed in a basin as described above. Large prints can be washed in the flat type of developing-dish, provided that the flow of water is vigorous enough to ensure that the heavy hypo fluid does not remain stagnant at the bottom of the dish, and provided that the prints are turned over from time to time during the operation, so as to ensure that they do not stick together and hinder diffusion of the hypo from the prints into the water. Several dishes may be arranged in cascade form as in Fig. 23. The prints straight from the fixing-bath are placed in the lower dish, and after ten minutes moved up to the next tier, being replaced in the bottom one by other prints from the fixing-bath. After another ten minutes they are again moved up one tier, and a new lot of prints is put in the bottom tier. At the end of a further ten minutes the top section are properly washed, and this operation can go on until all the prints have been treated.

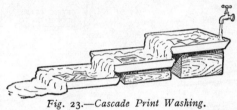

Fig. 23.—Cascade Print Washing.

Precaution should be taken to ensure that the water does not carry the prints over the edges of the dishes or compartments and down on to the drain-hole of the sink, otherwise there may be a flood, due to overflowing of the sink.

DRYING

When the prints are removed from washing, as much excess water as possible should be extracted from them. A good plan is to spread them out on one-half of a good, fluffless towel, using the other half to mop up the water from the backs and fronts of the prints. Alternatively, they can be mopped with a piece of viscose sponge. Photographic blotting-paper may be used, but *on no account* must ordinary blotting-paper be used in conjunction with photographic prints, as it contains hypo.

The prints may be pinned up by one corner in

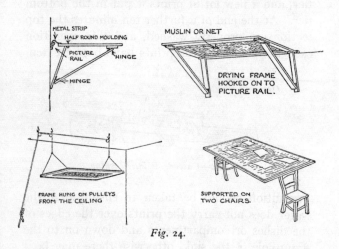

METAL STRIP
HALF ROUND MOULDING
PICTURE RAIL
HINGE
HINGE

MUSLIN OR NET

DRYING FRAME
HOOKED ON TO
PICTURE RAIL.

FRAME HUNG ON PULLEYS
FROM THE CEILING

SUPPORTED ON
TWO CHAIRS.

Fig. 24.

some convenient place to dry, but a much better plan is to prepare a simple wooden frame measuring, say, 4 feet × 2 feet, and to cover this with muslin or cheesecloth free from dressing. This is suspended in a horizontal position so that air can reach *both sides* of the muslin, and prints are laid upon it *face downwards*. They will then dry free from dust, and will not curl up so badly as they do when pinned up (Fig. 24).

GLAZING

Prints on glossy surface paper can be dried in the manner described above, but if the full effect of the glossy surface is to be obtained, the prints should be " glazed ". This consists of drying them in close contact with a flat, shining surface such as a sheet of plate glass, or a chromium or ferrotype glazing sheet. This surface must be prepared first by very thorough cleaning, and then by treatment with a suitable medium. Plate glass can be given a preliminary polish with french chalk. Either glass or ferrotype plates can be prepared by polishing with a solution of sixty grains of white wax in 3 ozs. of benzol used with a pad of soft cloth. The layer of wax should be made as thin as possible by thorough rubbing. A proprietary glazing solution can be used or artists' liquid extract of ox-gall. Chromium-plated surfaces do not need such a preparation. The thoroughly wet print is laid face downwards on the surface of the glazing sheet, and a roller squeegee is applied to the back to press the print in intimate contact with the frame and exclude excess water. When the print is first laid down, a piece of absorbent material can be laid over it to soak up this water as it is squeezed out. When laying down large prints, work outwards from the centre if your squeegee is a small one, and give the final strokes to the bare back of the print. When drying glazed prints, do not attempt to hurry with heat, or the prints will become stuck to the plate, and it will be impossible to remove them without destroying them. If correctly prepared, they should themselves come away from the glazing sheet, but if they seem a little slow, one corner of the print may be gently lifted with the finger, when it should strip off without further trouble.

TRIMMING

Prints will generally be made with white edges, and if they are properly placed on to ready-cut paper, nothing more need be done. If made on larger sheets, they will probably need final trimming. A proper trimmer is the best thing for the job, although it can be done with a very sharp knife and a steel straight-edge.

CHAPTER IX

ENLARGING

PROJECTION PRINTING

THE printing methods previously described produce a print of exactly the same size as the original negative. If you wish to make a print of the whole or part of the negative to be of a size different

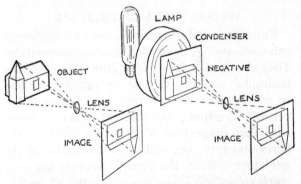

Fig. 25.—Comparison between Camera and Enlarger.

from that of the original, then this work is done in the " enlarger ". Its more accurate modern name is the projection printer, and in such an apparatus you can make pictures smaller as well as larger than the original negative.

The principle of enlarging is the same as that of taking a picture (Fig. 25). If you put your camera up in front of a landscape, the light-rays from the subject passing through the lens are projected on to the sensitive material to make a negative. If you put a negative in the enlarger, it is for all practical purposes in the position of the subject, and the light-rays from it, passing through the lens, are projected on to the sensitive surface to give you a positive print. The fact that the print is larger than the negative, whereas in the camera the record is smaller than the subject, does not alter the underlying principle.

SEVERAL KINDS OF ENLARGER

Enlargers are of two main classes : (a) condenser enlargers, and (b) those with diffused illumination. They can further be divided into two types, the horizontal and the vertical, so called according to whether the beam travels in a horizontal or vertical direction. Until recent years an overwhelming proportion of enlargers were of the horizontal type, but with the introduction of the miniature camera, the vertical enlarger has very much come into its own. It has the advantage that it does not require much bench space, which is an important consideration, while it can be worked from one spot without the operator having to walk up and down. The whole of the component parts are suspended on one pillar or girder, thus making for accuracy of alignment, and, finally, it is an advantage for the surface of the printing-paper to be horizontal. Against this, the horizontal enlarger has rather a low market value at the present time, so that the beginner may be able to pick up second-hand apparatus inexpensively.

AUTOMATIC FOCUSING

A refinement which is possessed by certain of the vertical enlargers is automatic focusing. In the ordinary way, when the degree of enlargement is altered, the image does not remain in focus, and this sometimes causes a considerable amount of manipulation when a precise degree of enlargement is required. In the automatic-focusing type of enlarger, an arm or link moves against a curved plate or slot as the body of the enlarger is moved up and down the supporting pillar and automatically keeps the picture in focus all the time.

OTHER REFINEMENTS

The bodies of many vertical enlargers are counterbalanced by means of a weight on a cord running over a pulley, and very little force is required to move them up and down. Most of the better-class horizontal enlargers possess a swinging negative holder which enables the user to correct distortion caused by incorrect positioning of the camera during exposure. Vertical enlargers, except in one or two cases, do not have this facility, but there is available a type of base-board which is free to rotate in all directions around a central ball joint and which serves the same purpose.

LIGHT SOURCES

The illumination which is almost universal is electric light, and even in places where current is not available, effective work has been done with car-batteries and a suitable voltage lamp. In earlier days, incandescent-gas mantles were used in the diffuser type of enlarger, and, at the other end of the scale, the carbon arc has been used for high-power work. A small low-pressure mercury vapour tube in rectangular form is used in big enlargers for professional work, and some work has been done with high-pressure mercury-vapour discharge lamps.

CONDENSER ENLARGERS

The condenser type of enlarger consists of a light-source of a small size, and of as high an intensity as is possible within reasonable limits; in front of this is a condenser; the negative close to it; and finally the projection lens. The condenser usually consists of two plano-convex lenses of fairly short focus with the convex sides facing one another and nearly touching. Such a condenser has a diameter a little larger than the diagonal of the largest negative with which it is to be used. Its function is to collect as much of the light-rays as possible and lead them to the projection lens, while at the same time ensuring that an evenly illuminated image of the negative shall be projected on to the enlarging surface.

DIFFUSER ENLARGERS

The diffuser type of enlarger consists of a large white or similar surface which is strongly lit from sources which are otherwise hidden. The light reflected from the diffusing surface passes through the negative, thence to the lens, and then to the enlarging surface.

While the condenser enlarger gives the maximum degree of light from a given source, and a very crisp result, it gives a much more contrasty one, and any faults or blemishes or grain which are present in the negative tend to be exaggerated. The diffuser type of enlarger gives a slightly softer and more mellow picture, and at the same time any incidental faults and retouching work do not show up so badly.

DIFFUSION-CONDENSER ENLARGERS

The modern miniature camera negative presents a special problem, because while the large degree of magnification demands relatively high intensity in the light, it also requires that any scratches or blemishes should not be emphasised. This is overcome in most cases by using a condenser system backed by an illuminant in the form of an opal electric lamp. The condenser ensures the maximum use of the light, while the large, even light-source destroys harshness that would otherwise be present.

LENSES

It is just as important that the lens of the enlarger should be a good one as in the case of the camera. It need not be so highly corrected for colour as the camera lens, and consequently need not be so expensive. In certain cases the camera lens is used with the enlarger, particularly in miniature work, but it does not necessarily follow that a lens which is perfect for the camera is also perfect for the enlarger, while one which may be somewhat unsatisfactory for camera work may work perfectly in the enlarger.

An inexpensive makeshift which has been used with considerable success is to fix up a box with a condenser at the front end, and a suitable light behind it, and to mount in front of the condenser a camera of the folding bellows type, preferably an old plate-camera, a plate-holder being modified to act as a negative carrier.

WORKING ARRANGEMENTS

In setting up the enlarger in the dark-room, it should be kept away from the sink. A good arrangement is to have the developing-dish a little to the right of the enlarger, followed by the rinsing-dish and the fixing-dish at reasonable intervals, the latter adjacent to the dark-room sink. The dark-room clock, for timing exposures and development, should be placed near the enlarger. Absolute cleanliness is necessary when enlarging, as any dirt on the negative, or even on the condenser, will also be enlarged, while dirt on the enlarger lens will possibly cause scatter, and consequent light fogging. The optical parts of the enlarger should be cleaned gently with a piece of well-washed soft linen. Do not use silk, as this merely electrifies the glass parts and causes them to attract yet more dirt. The negative itself can be dusted with a soft brush such as an artist's mop.

FOCUSING

Very many enlargements are spoiled by bad focusing in the enlarger, of which the worker is often unaware because of the comparatively low light intensity of the projected image. If the negative is too dense, or the image is too dark to allow you to focus with ease, remove it and *place in exactly the same plane* a focusing negative. This can conveniently consist of a fogged and developed plate or film on which scratches or cuts through the emulsion have been made. If this is focused sharply on the easel, the actual negative will also be focused sharply.

ASCERTAINING EXPOSURE

It is impossible to give any indication as to exposure, as this depends on so many factors— *e.g.*, the density of the negative, the degree of enlargement, the type of illumination, and so on. It is unnecessary, however, to waste large quantities of paper making blind guesses as to the exposure. The correct plan is to make an exposure test-strip. Most packets of large-sized paper contain an additional sheet or sheets of test material. A long strip is laid on the base-

board on the easel of the enlarger so that it goes
where the most important portions of the negative
are being projected. The illuminant is turned
out or the cap placed on the enlarger lens while
this is being done. The operation is facilitated
if a transparent orange cap is used, because while
the projected orange image will be visible, it
cannot affect the paper. The strip is held down
by some convenient means and is then given a
series of " stepped " exposures. Each exposure
can, with advantage, be twice as long as the
previous one. For example, the whole strip is
first given an exposure of two seconds. With a
piece of opaque card, a 1-inch section at the end
is then covered, and at the end of another two
seconds the card is moved forward another inch.
It is then held in position for four seconds, moved
up another inch, and so on. The final result will
be that progressive sections of the strip will have
received exposures of two, four, eight, and
sixteen seconds. The strip is then developed for
an exact two minutes (or whatever the correct
developing time may be for the particular paper
and formula), rinsed and fixed, and then examined
under white light, care first being taken to cover
up all other sensitive material that may be in the
dark-room. It will be easy to select which is the
correct exposure, while if there should happen to
be no exposure which is quite correct on the strip,
it will indicate in which direction further experiments should be carried.

ORTHOCHROMATIC

The two accompanying pictures show the colour rendering given by Orthochromatic and Panchromatic films and plates. Note that in both cases the yellow objects are well recorded, but that the Ortho. or Chrome film gives an unduly light version of the blue car and an unduly dark version of the red car. The relative brilliance of the colours as shown in the panchromatic picture is closely similar to the actual visual appearance.

COLOUR KEY

PANCHROMATIC

This photograph was taken on a " chrome " film without a filter. The sky area is white and without interest.

This photograph was taken on the same type of film, but a yellow filter was placed in front of the lens.   Note how the clouds give added interest to the sky.

VARIABLE CONTROL OF EXPOSURE

An advantage which is associated with enlarging is the fact that the distance between the negative and the printing-paper allows of the interposition of various masks and other devices to secure particular effects. If, for example, the sky portion of a negative is so strongly exposed that it still remains white when the landscape portion is fully printed in the enlarging, then a mask may be cut roughly to the shape of the foreground, and held over the foreground during enlargement, being moved gently to and fro to avoid any danger of a hard edge. This will permit a longer exposure of the sky portion. Another dodge is to cut a small circular hole in a large piece of card, and use this to isolate a beam of light on to some small but particularly dense part of the projected negative image. The image can also be " vignetted "—that is, a part of it caused to die away to whiteness with a soft edge by placing a shaped mask, preferably with the edge cut with saw-shaped teeth about half an inch deep, about half-way between the lens and the paper.

PATTERNED SCREENS

It is possible to obtain screens which are placed on the surface of the printing-paper and give the enlargement a grained, etched, or linen-texture effect. They are sometimes useful for great degrees of enlargement.

E—PHOTO

DIFFUSION

Other effects may be obtained by diffusing the image with what is known as " bolting silk " which is obtainable from your photographic dealer. It should be stretched in a frame and laid touching, or almost touching, the paper, and will produce a very pleasant effect in which the hard lines of the subject are surrounded with a slightly fogged " aura ", giving a suave and mysterious appearance to the picture. A similar effect may be produced by using a diffusion disc on the lens of the enlarger. Such discs generally consist of optically flat glass with wavy lines, concentric circles, or irregular patterns engraved or raised upon them. These allow the greater part of the rays to pass through them unmodified, but gently scatter a small proportion of them.

MULTIPLE PRINTING

A number of quite amusing tricks are possible. For example, if you have a portrait of a person in an uninteresting background, and a negative of a suitable background, it is possible to place one within the other. An easy way of doing this is to paint around the figure of the person on the negative with a suitable opaque medium, such as " Photopake ". Then a very dense enlargement of the figure *only* is made to the correct size. This is cut out with scissors, and, if necessary, reinforced with an application of " Photopake ". The " background " negative is then put in the enlarger and projected to a suitable size. The paper to be printed on is placed in position, and the dense image of the person placed on the paper in the position that it is required the person shall occupy. The background is then exposed without moving either the paper or the mask, the portrait negative is put into the enlarger, and its projected image made to fit the mask which is already in position. This is, of course, done with the orange transparent cap on the lens. The mask is then removed and the image exposed. The sheet of paper is then developed. Subsequently any tiny discrepancies in the joining of the figure and the background can be covered by re-touching.

ENLARGED NEGATIVES

One of the disadvantages of really small negatives is the difficulty of re-touching them, as even the finest pencil- or brush-strokes would be relatively enormous, or coarse, when enlarged. This can be avoided by making an enlarged negative. To do this a transparency has first to be made. A lantern-plate is quite suitable, and the positive can be made by contact printing. Development should be short, and while the shadows are of reasonable density, the highlights should also have a well-defined tone. The positive is then enlarged again on to a suitable plate or film of the " ordinary " slow-speed type. Plates should preferably be used for this purpose, but they must be of the backed type, as otherwise you may encounter trouble with halation.

SUITABLE PAPERS

As has been mentioned above, the comparatively fast bromide papers are most suitable for enlarging, and the rough or semi-rough surfaces will be found best in cases where the original negative is enlarged a considerable number of diameters. Cream as well as white papers may be obtained, and in some cases these are preferable for enlarged images. This is particularly so in the case of chloro-bromide papers, some of the modern varieties of these papers being of sufficient rapidity to be used in the enlarger without requiring unduly long exposures. The man who does enlarging must be prepared on occasion to give relatively long times of exposure, and for this reason the truly safe character of the dark-room illumination is of extreme importance. If the intensity of the projected image is so low that the paper has to be kept exposed for a considerable period, it may give an opportunity for other light in the room to act upon the paper and fog it.

TESTING DARK-ROOM LIGHTING

Little leakages of light into the room then become important, as does also the really safe character of the dark-room safe light. If there is any doubt, a test can be made by exposing to the dark-room illumination for a long period a piece of paper with an opaque object placed in the centre of it. If development reveals a silhouette of the object, however faint, then the lighting is not safe. It must also be borne in mind that the enlarger itself may be the source of the trouble. If the light within it is not properly trapped, with the consequence that unwanted light leaks out at various parts of the instrument, it may be necessary to shroud the enlarger with a dark cloth during the longer exposures, but do not interfere unduly with ventilation, or the enlarger lamp-house may become excessively hot, burn or crack the negative, and possibly blow the lamp.

SIZE REDUCTION AND LANTERN SLIDES

I mentioned earlier that it is possible to make reduced-size pictures, as well as enlargements, through the so-called enlarger. It is not often that the photographer will wish to do this work on paper, but we mention the method because it is recognised to be probably the finest way of obtaining lantern slides of first-class quality. In fact, it is claimed in some quarters that even though the slide is the same size as the negative, a projection print of it will be better than a contact print. The lantern plates used for this purpose must be backed, otherwise there will be halation troubles. There is no doubt that the lantern slide is again coming into its own, as people recognise more and more the beauty of the results which can be obtained.

CHAPTER X

"SNAPS" OR PHOTOGRAPHS?

THE fact that you are reading this book shows that you are not content to be a mere snapshotter who knows nothing about the underlying principles of the photographs he takes; but the ability to take pictures which are properly exposed, properly developed, and well printed and enlarged is not all that is necessary. There are many people who can draw, but comparatively few artists. There are many people who take photographs, but only a few whose pictures are a source of genuine delight to their friends as well as themselves. To go thoroughly into the question of what makes one photograph outstanding, and another, although equally as competent, dull and uninteresting would take a further complete book, and here I can only refer briefly to one or two points. If, however, my remarks can give the photographer some idea of the things that he should practise and study, they will have served their purpose.

FILTERS

Get to know the uses of filters. Even the ordinary haphazard snap is improved if the sky has a grey tone and perhaps white clouds, instead of being just white paper. Yellow filters on ortho-chromatic, and medium-green filters on panchro-matic film will give a truthful rendering of sub-jects, but experiment also with deep green and red and orange filters with which to secure ex-aggerated and dramatic effects. The rule is, that if you wish to make an object appear light in your picture, you use a filter of its own colour, but if you wish to render the record of it dark, you use a filter which is its opposite. For example, if the subject is red flowers among green foliage, a green filter will make the photograph of the foliage pale, and of the flower dark, while a red filter will make the picture of the flower appear nearly white, and the foliage dark. A yellow flower would not be greatly affected by either colour filter, as yellow is very largely a mixture of red light and green light.

VIEWING FILTERS

These are filters through which the photographer observes the scene. They give the approximate photographic effect and enable the effects of other filters to be tried visually. Viewing filters are *not* used on the camera.

LIGHTING

Learn to observe the direction of the light in relation to the subject (see Fig. 26). The effect can be observed very well on an octagonal church spire. If the light is shining in direction 1, the subject will look flat and without form. Bushes, houses, and people will look like flat pieces of cut-out paper. With the light shining in direction 2 or 3, the subject will take on depth of form, but about half of it will appear in shadow, and the

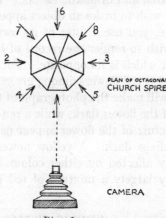

PLAN OF OCTAGONAL
CHURCH SPIRE

CAMERA

Fig. 26.
Arrows indicate the direction of lighting.

general effect will be one of high contrast. If it shines from 4 and 5, we get a very pleasant form of lighting. There will be a little shadow on the side away from the light, the side nearest to the light will be brilliant, and between these two extremes there will be a range of grey tones which will show to the fullest degree the form and texture of the objects being recorded. Directions 6, 7, and 8 indicate the position if you are photographing " against the light ". It will be very difficult to get a picture under condition 6, except at or about the time of sunset, with the sun obscured or partly obscured by clouds or some solid object. Alternatively, near the middle of the day, when the light is shining from a high angle, some interesting effects may be secured. With the light coming from the angle 7 and 8 (or from 6, with the sun high up), the effect will be of a glistening line of light round the edge of the subject. The side of the object facing the photographer will only be lit by reflection, and the exposure will have to be increased probably four times above normal for the type of subject in order to obtain a record of the shadow details. For portraiture, additional lighting can be cast into the shadows by the use of large white-painted boards or sheets, or even sheets of newspaper, used as reflectors. This technique is similar to that used by the professional cinematographer.

Rather more complex is the business of taking photographs in artificial light, and is dealt with in Chapter XIII, p. 165, should you wish to experiment with this type of work.

NATURALISM

A lot of your pictures will be portrait snaps of your friends and relatives. Try to make them as real as possible. Avoid the stiff and waxwork effects which are produced by so many amateurs. Many people, when they know that they are going to have their photograph taken, have a habit of standing stiff and straight, and either staring into the camera or grinning in an inane manner, or they indulge in foolish antics to cover their feelings of embarrassment.

Learn little tricks to put them at their ease. Take photographs without telling them you are doing so, or, if you are forced to arrange them, try to interest them in your conversation, and snap them as they relax. Some of my best photographs of groups of people have been secured after I had " taken " the photograph. If your subject is engaged in a familiar occupation —e.g., a man lighting his pipe, or a woman cutting flowers from the garden—you will secure a more natural picture.

APERTURE AND FOCUSING

If you work at a small aperture, nearly every-thing in the picture will be sharp and well defined. This may be good record photography, but is not often artistically pleasing. If you open the aperture of the lens, some parts of the picture, both behind or in front of the point focused upon, will become softened, and the details will run together. In extreme cases the details will be entirely lost, and the form will be rendered dif-fused, until it may become difficult to recognise it.

DIFFERENTIAL FOCUSING

This gives a valuable power of selection. For example, an object in the foreground may be rendered sharp against a hazy background, and will thus stand out more readily. This device is often used in photography, but care should be taken not to place your subject in front of trees or foliage through which light is shining, otherwise the background in the photograph will be covered by white circular blobs. In some cases it may be desirable that a part of the middle distance, or even the background, should be sharper than objects in the foreground. The selection of the plane of sharpest focus according to the needs of the picture is known as " differential focusing ".

FOREGROUND OBJECTS

Learn the value of objects in or near the foreground, particularly in landscape work. When you look at an actual landscape you observe it with two eyes. A large number of factors, including its actual dimensions in relation to yourself, the colour, and the atmosphere give you a sense of grandeur and distance. If you photograph the landscape as it is, it will often be completely disappointing. You are seeing through only one " eye "—the lens—and the picture is small. The distant hills will have become thin grey lines only a few inches long, while the rolling lands in between are just a series of intermittent greys. If, however, an archway, a balustrade, an iron grille, a branch of a tree, or something similar in the foreground is included to form part of your picture, it will not only help to frame it in an interesting way, but will also immediately give a feeling of size and distance to the picture, largely because of its vigorous tones in relation to the more delicate ones of the distant details.

PERSPECTIVE

A drawing or photograph in which the form, shape, and arrangement appear exactly the same as the actual object does to the eye of the observer is said to be " in perspective ". The word means " look through ", and it is as if one were looking at the subject through a window, the light-rays at the window surface then being permanently " frozen " on to the glass to form a picture. No picture is in wrong perspective provided it is looked at from the correct *viewpoint*, but the viewing distance from the photograph should be relatively the same as the original distance of the camera from the subject, if exactly the same effect is to be secured. This rule is not altered by the focal length of the camera lens that may be used. If, for instance, a man 6 *feet* high is photographed by a camera 20 *feet* away, and the photograph when printed shows him 6 *inches* high, then the photograph should be viewed at a distance of 20 *inches*. In practical fact there is a considerable amount of latitude, but if the rule is violently broken, the picture will appear to be distorted. For example, if you photograph your man from a distance of 10 *feet*, the photograph should be viewed from a distance of 10 *inches*. Viewing the picture from twice or three times this distance would not matter if he were standing upright, but if, as is so often the case, he were taken sitting in a chair with one leg over the other and a foot towards you, the effect would be grotesque in the

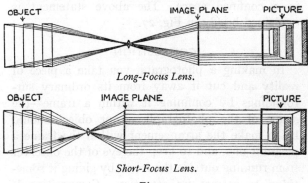

Long-Focus Lens.

Short-Focus Lens.

Fig. 27.

extreme, the foot appearing huge as compared with the head and body.

On the other hand, you may sometimes see in public cinemas, news pictures taken down the length of a cricket pitch, in which the pitch appears to be only a few feet long, instead of its correct 22 yards. This is because the picture has been taken through a lens of tremendously long focus from an enormous distance. Even that member of the audience in the cinema who is sitting in the back row is insufficiently far away from the screen to get a view of the picture which is correct in perspective. Although this is not a great defect, a practised eye can soon detect the really long-focus picture.

On the other hand, the short-focus lens, used closer to the principal object, can be very usefully employed to give an illusion of size and distance in a confined space. The above statement is explained briefly in Fig. 27.

COMPOSITION

In making a photograph you take a piece of reality and cut it away from its ordinary surroundings by confining it within a frame—the shape of the photograph. Your object should be to make the arrangement within the frame a pleasant one, and to keep the eye of the observer from running outside the frame by giving it something to attract its attention. Composition is the arrangement of the pattern of the " lines " and tones within the picture. For example, the line from the hand up around the arm and shoulders of a person will help to lead the eye to the face, which is the main part of the picture. A " line " need not necessarily be a continuous one, and in fact in a photograph actual lines are seldom present. They are formed by the edges between two tones or by the occurrence of several similar tones in regular arrangement which form an imaginary line.

If the composition lines in a picture are straight and long, and nearly horizontal and vertical, the

Water Scene.

The Same, with Foreground Interest Added.

Decreasing Ovals.

Radiating Straight Lines.

Long, Flowing Lines, mostly Vertical, make for Dignity and Calm.

Short, Irregular Lines make for restlessness.

High View Point.

Low View Point.

Fig. 28.

effect will be of calmness. Long, flowing, curved shapes will have much of this effect. On the other hand, short, abrupt lines tending in various directions will keep a feeling of restlessness. Examples of these two opposite subjects are : a picture of a castle reflected in cloudy water, and the jagged irregular effect produced by rocks and the broken spray of a wave dashing on the shore. Lines radiating from a point in the picture will lead the eye to that point—as, for example, a view down a path or stream. Concentric ovals give an interesting effect. An example of this is a view down a valley with large hills receding into the background.

The separation of the picture into planes or areas going back into the distance is quite important. The rich tones of the foreground, behind this the medium tones of the middle distance, backed up again by the grey tones of the background, can be used to great effect if an attempt is made to understand them.

The would-be pictorial photographer is advised to study the works of painters in the leading museums and picture-galleries.

CHOOSING THE VIEWPOINT

The great difference between the artist and the photographer is the ability of the former to leave out what is superfluous in the scene before him and, if necessary, to re-arrange what is left. The photographer must take what his camera sees.

He can, however, exercise considerable control upon the arrangement by choosing a suitable viewpoint. Do not photograph a subject from the point from which you first see it, but walk up and down to see if a better arrangement can be obtained from an adjacent position.

TRIMMING

Your subject may not entirely suit the shape of your negative, or you may have to take a much

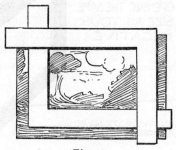

Fig. 29

larger area than you really require. This can be rectified on the print, particularly if you have an enlarger, by selecting the shape and arrangement that you desire, and either trimming away the rest or masking it off when you make your enlargement. An excellent accessory is simply made from two L-shaped pieces of card (see Fig. 29), which are moved over the surface of a trial print to enclose more or less of the area, as you require. It is sometimes of assistance to carry with you a piece of card with a central hole the same shape as your negative, and a piece of string knotted through the card, and of such length that if the eye is placed at its extremity it will cover the same angle through the aperture in the card as is covered by the camera lens. This can be used as a viewer in selecting pictures before

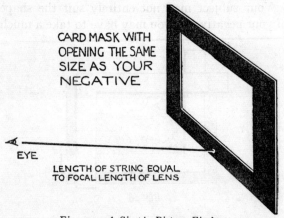

CARD MASK WITH OPENING THE SAME SIZE AS YOUR NEGATIVE

EYE

LENGTH OF STRING EQUAL TO FOCAL LENGTH OF LENS

Fig. 30.—A Simple Picture Finder.

making your exposure, and also to train yourself in " seeing " possible pictures.

HIGH KEY, LOW KEY AND COLOUR

The mood of a picture is greatly affected by the manner in which it is printed. A delicate subject, such as a child picture, printed in light, delicate, cool, grey tones on white paper, obviously makes a striking contrast to a dramatic picture with rich, heavy tones and shadows, printed in rich brownish-black tones on cream-coloured paper. The first picture may be on a paper with a fine eggshell texture, and the latter on something which is rough and rugged, in keeping with the subject.

Bromide paper will give the cool effect, and for those who wish to go to the extra trouble there are many other processes which will give exquisitely delicate results.

Chloro-bromide paper will give rich brown tones, which can also be obtained by means of the carbro process. Carbro will also give a whole range of different colours, which are appropriate for different types of picture, but should not be overdone. Toning will also give you a range of different colours.

The working up of prints with chalk and pigment, water-colour and oil-colour, are subjects outside the scope of this book, but offer considerable interest to the photographic worker.

MOUNTING

Pictures can be made or marred by the mounting of them. Use good quality mounting-board, do not use fancy colours, and keep the type of mounting simple. The print should be placed slightly above the centre of the board, otherwise it will appear to be below the centre. The print can be finished with a white edge, and mounted so that this is immediately surrounded by a narrow grey line formed by a sheet of "tint" paper.

Another good plan is to rule a black pencil line all around the print about $\frac{1}{4}$ inch or $\frac{1}{2}$ inch away from it. Never allow the mounting to become more important than the picture itself.

CHAPTER XI

COLOUR PHOTOGRAPHY

THROUGHOUT the history of the development of photography there has been a constant search for a successful means of recording colour. Many methods were proposed but it was not until emulsion-making techniques reached their present state of excellence that colour photography became a practical proposition for everybody.

Two basic methods were feasible, the " additive " and the " subtractive ". In the former the picture was generally built from tiny colour elements of the primary colours, red, green and blue (examples were Dufaycolor, Lumière Alticolor and the Johnson Colour Screen Process based on an older method called Finlay).

The " subtractive " process is the one which has been most fully developed and is the basis of all the present-day materials. The image is formed of dyes in three continuous colour layers, with the addition, in some cases, of a control filter layer. The complementaries of the three primary colours are used, that is, cyan (blue-green) magenta and yellow. The function is to act as controls for the red, green and blue light, leaving the eye to observe the effect in the form of a colour transparency. Typical examples are Agfacolor, Anscocolor, Ektachrome, Ferraniacolor, Gevacolor, Ilfochrome and Kodachrome II.

In addition to the reversal process, which provides a transparency, there are negative-positive processes such as Agfacolor, Ektacolor, Ferraniacolor, Gevacolor, Ilfocolor, Kodacolor, etc., in which the negative film has three dye layers similar to those in the reversal material. The negative film is then printed, either by contact or by projection (enlarging), on to a similar type of three-layer emulsion coated upon a white paper or plastic base, to give a colour " print ".

Transparencies can be examined in a small hand " viewer ", often containing its own battery lighting, projected on to the back of a small translucent screen, or forwards on to a larger white opaque screen.

EXPOSURE

Although colour films used generally to be somewhat slower than most black-and-white films, the latest types of emulsion are as " fast " as many panchromatic materials. Image quality and colour rendering have been vastly improved, although greater care in exposing them in comparison with black-and-white is still essential. It should also be remembered that three distinct and separate images have to be maintained in correct relationship to one another. As accurate an estimate as possible must be made of the exposure required: an exposure meter is therefore generally advisable, although complete reliance may be placed upon the exposure-tables provided with the film by most makers.

Exposure errors which are tolerable in black-and-white photography may ruin a colour shot. It is sometimes possible to resort to after-treatment for unrepeatable pictures, but the result is generally less good than would be obtained with correct exposure. There is usually greater latitude with the negative–positive process than there is with the reversal process.

CHOICE OF SUBJECT

The tendency will be for colour photographers to choose strong, brilliant subjects and to work on very bright days. While the bright colours make attractive pictures, due regard should be had for the rules of composition in placing these colours in the picture-frame, and quite pleasing pictures can be taken of quietly coloured subjects.

Brilliant sunshine is not necessarily the best light for colour photography. The brilliant high lights and heavy shadows make a high degree of contrast, which may possibly be outside the scope of the material to render correctly. The ideal lighting is obtained on a sunlit day with large masses of white cloud present in the sky, or on a bright day with the sky very slightly obscured. Then the whole subject is much more evenly lit, and plenty of light is being reflected into the shadows.

Any subject which is receiving coloured light—*e.g.*, reflection from a blue sky or from a red brick wall—will show that colour in its shadows, and the colour camera has an uncomfortable habit of slightly stressing such phenomena, which are always present, and which are seen by the eye, but are rarely apprehended by the mind.

ARTIFICIAL LIGHT

The colour of the picture will be strongly influenced by the colour of the light in which the photograph was taken. If artificial light is used, then the photographer must either adopt material which has been specially sensitised and balanced for that type of light, or use filters over the lens of his camera which will modify the light before it reaches the film.

VIEWING

The best method of viewing is by projection, and this is made easy because there is a wide variety of equipment from which to choose, from small compact units of relatively low power to large and powerful instruments suitable for use in public halls. The larger models are often cooled by built-in motor-driven blowers.

There are also on the market a number of viewing-boxes which enable the transparencies to be viewed individually, in most cases under a lens which not only magnifies but also gives a greater sense of depth and modelling to the picture. Such magnification is particularly necessary when examining colour transparencies taken with miniature cameras. These viewers generally provide that the light from the sky, or from an artificial source, shall be reflected upwards from a surface so as to pass through the transparency and then proceed to the eye of the observer.

COLOUR PRINTS

Earlier processes of colour printing used to involve the making of three separate negatives through " tri-colour " discriminating filters in each of the primary colours, red, green and blue. But, as has been stated, modern three-layer colour negative emulsions have greatly simplified the processes in making colour prints on paper.

COLOUR PROJECTION

The least expensive form of colour transparency is that made on 35-mm.-width material, usually in the size 24 mm. × 36 mm. (approx.: 1 inch × 1½ inches). There are many types of projection equipment available for showing these " miniature " slides—they are usually referred to as " 2 by 2 " because the slides themselves, either in the form of cardboard mounts, metal-framed glazed mounts or simple bound sandwiches of pairs of glasses, measure 2 inches by 2 inches.

The projection of colour transparencies is also now greatly simplified by the introduction of fully automatic projectors remotely controlled by push-buttons. Recorded commentaries on the series of slides to be shown can be made with the aid of syn-chronised tape-recording/reproducing equipment.

To cater for the photographer with a camera which makes 12 pictures on 120 size film (nominal 2¼ inches square) projectors are now available for transparencies of this size.

CHAPTER XII

CINEMATOGRAPHY

NARROW-GAUGE FILMS

THE film used by amateurs is known as narrow-gauge, because it is smaller in size than the standard 35-mm.-width material used by the professional. Film is described by its overall width, and the three most popular amateur sizes are 16 mm., 9·5 mm., and 8 mm.

WHY PICTURES "MOVE"

A moving-picture camera is a very tiny camera which takes a series of photographs very rapidly one after the other on a long strip of film. When the complete film is put in a machine which shows these pictures one after another, the fact that there are slight progressive differences between the successive photographs gives an illusion of movement. This is due to the fact that when the eye observes anything, the impression takes a fraction of time to die out even after the object has been removed. When the film is shown at such a speed that the new picture is placed on the screen before the impression of the old one has died, the observer imagines the continuous presence of a single picture which moves.

CAMERA MECHANISM

Nearly all the space in a movie camera is taken up with storing the film before and after it is exposed. An amateur movie camera consists of a train of mechanism driven by a clockwork motor which (*a*) feeds the unexposed film to the actual point of exposure, (*b*) pulls the film down in jerks past the exposure point, and (*c*) stores the film again after exposure. A movie camera film has a series of holes perforated down its length, these holes enabling it to be moved with precision by the camera mechanism.

HOW FILM IS SUPPLIED

There are two methods of storing film in the camera, and film is supplied to suit these :—

(a) *The Daylight Loading Spool.*—This is a solid-sided spool. Film is wound on this, and when the spool is full the film is contained between the solid flanges and several turns of an opaque material of the same width as the film, which is fixed to its two outer ends. In this state the full spool is safe to handle *with care* in daylight. In the camera the unexposed film is wound off one spool, passes the exposure point in the camera, and is then coiled on to a second spool.

(b) *The Charger or Cassette.*—This consists of a container divided into two light-tight chambers. The film is able to pass from the top chamber through a chute to the outside of the cassette, then past the exposure point of the camera, and in through another chute to the bottom chamber, where the exposed film is taken up and stored.

THE EXPOSURE POINT

At the point where the exposures are made, the film is held flat in the correct position between two flat plates of metal which bear down on the surfaces of the film. The metal plate nearest the lens is pierced with an aperture which is the size of the picture. The actual contact with the film is reduced to the minimum by cutting away the surfaces of the two plates, leaving only narrow " rails " to support the film. The two halves of the mechanism are kept in contact with the film by gentle spring pressure. This mechanism is known as the " gate ". The film is held stationary in the gate during exposure, but immediately after each exposure is pulled downwards the depth of one picture by an intermittent mechanism, which consists generally of a claw which enters a perforation in the film, remains in the perforation and carries the film with it on its downward stroke, but withdraws from the perforation before it makes its upward stroke. The shutter of the camera, which is generally a revolving disc or an oscillating plate, obscures the lens while the film is moving downwards, and uncovers it while the film is stationary. The shutter, the claw, and the other mechanism for moving the film through the camera are all linked together.

EXPOSURE TIME AND APERTURE

The cine camera generally exposes pictures at the rate of sixteen per second, the exposure time for each picture being about one-thirty-second of a second. The exposure time remains constant as long as the speed of the film remains constant. It is therefore the custom to control the exposure by varying only the aperture of the lens. This single control has made possible " auto " cameras in which the iris is photo-cell-operated.

Allowance must, however, be made if the speed of the camera movement is altered. If the film takes twice as long to pass through the camera, then each individual picture receives twice the exposure time. This must be compensated by closing down the lens.

PROJECTION

A similar apparatus is necessary to show the pictures. A cine-projector is very much like a tiny enlarger or magic lantern, with means for storing film before and after showing, and for passing it through the gate. The film is carried on spools of much larger size than are used in the camera. The film is drawn off the top spool by a sprocket or toothed wheel, and is fed to the gate, where it is pulled down intermittently, and then proceeds to another sprocket, and then on to the take-up spool. The sprockets move continuously, and loose loops are left between them and the gate to allow for the intermittent movement in the gate. Most projectors use a claw to pull down the film in the gate, but other devices are also employed, which have their own advantages and disadvantages.

High-power incandescent electric lamps are used for projection, and a reflector and condenser system is employed, but it differs in detail from the system used in the condenser enlarger.

THE FILM

Although black-and-white panchromatic and super-panchromatic emulsions are available, by far the larger proportion of narrow-gauge film which is exposed is colour film, generally the same in type as the three-layer materials used by the still photographer.

Some of the film is developed by the ordinary negative and positive method, such as has been previously outlined, the main difference being that in this case, instead of a paper print or enlargement, the final positives are in the form of a series of images on a transparent strip of film.

THE REVERSAL PROCESS

By far the larger part of narrow-gauge film is, however, finished by the reversal process. You will remember that in Chapter IV I described how an exposed film was developed to give a metallic silver negative-image, after which the milky, unexposed emulsion which still remained in the film was dissolved away. The reversal process is a variation of this method. The exposed film is developed in the normal way to produce the metallic silver negative image. This is then dissolved away in a bleach or reversal bath. This process of bleaching does not affect the milky emulsion residue, which is then exposed to light and developed to give a positive image in which the subject is seen in its normal values. As an example, a negative image of a white handkerchief would be intensely black, while the black velvet upon which it lay would give rise to little or no negative image. If this image were bleached out, a clear space would be left to indicate the handkerchief, while almost the whole of the original emulsion would remain untouched at the place where the record of the black velvet occurred. If the film were now exposed to light, this emulsion could be developed to an intense black, and if we held the completed picture up against a white surface, we should see a white area representing the handkerchief, surrounded by blackness as in the original subject.

ADVANTAGES OF REVERSAL

The narrow-gauge film image is enlarged tremendously when it is projected. For example, the picture on 16-mm. film is enlarged over 190 times each way to give a picture 6 feet wide. The picture is made of tiny groups of silver grains, and these become apparent upon great magnification. In film which is processed by the reversal method the grain is considerably smaller than in film which has been printed from a negative. The quantity of film strip required is also halved.

It should be mentioned that all narrow-gauge cine film, in common with all film material for motion-pictures, is coated on a cellulose ester base, which is a slow-burning " safety base " material, virtually non-inflammable.

EXPOSURE

With negative material it is best, when in doubt as between the correctness of two exposures, to give the larger one, but, with reversal film, over-exposure should be avoided. If it occurs it means that so much of the sensitive emulsion is used up in making your negative that not sufficient is left to give a positive picture of good quality. On the other hand, a certain degree of under-exposure, which will give a dense picture, can afterwards be overcome by chemical reduction.

TECHNIQUE

The operations of manipulating a cine-camera should always be carried out in the same sequence, until they become instinctive, and the camera should always be fully wound after each " shot " or short series of shots.

Lighting follows the same rules as in ordinary photography, but you will find that what might be too hard for " still " pictures is quite satisfactory for moving ones.

On the other hand, in a case where a subject might be impossible to discern in a " still " picture, because it was flat and dark, movement would show its presence in a cine shot.

Filters are extremely valuable in movies, but it should be borne in mind that every shot is eventually shown as part of a film containing other shots, and it may appear extremely odd if some of these pictures have heavily filtered dark skies and clouds, and others are " bald-headed " and some are harsh and contrasty, while others are soft and diffused.

Shots should last from five to fifteen seconds, according to the interest of the subject. Do not attempt to cover a number of incidents from one viewpoint by using the camera like a fire-hose and spraying the scenery with it. Take the subjects as individual shots, stopping the camera before you move it. Until you are conversant with its use, it is much better to keep the camera absolutely still.

CINE COMPOSITION

Composition in cine work is different from ordinary composition, as movement within each part of the film and between different parts of the film has to be considered. A film consisting of a series of pictures, each of which is pictorially perfect, may be boring and uninteresting. Pictures which are individually less perfect will be much more satisfying if they have been made or edited in relation to one another.

EDITING

Editing is the name for cutting up and rearranging the individual shots to make a film.

F—PHOTO

" When in doubt, cut it out " is an excellent rule, although it needs some strength of character to follow it. Never hesitate to shorten the length of a shot. A sluggish film can be made to move fast by this method alone.

TITLING

Make titles for your films; make them terse but informative. Let them tell the audience about the shot which follows, but not about the next three or four shots that follow. Make them simple in design, and not over-elaborate. The main thing about a title is the wording in it. Decoration which obscures the wording makes a bad title. Keep your titles in the centre, and horizontal on the screen.

You can obtain ready-made titles from your photographic dealer. There is also a wide range of apparatus and sets of letters which will enable you to make and photograph your own.

PRESENTATION

Almost any fool can hang a screen and thread the film into the projector, but it is the wise man who realises that the presentation of the film is as important as the making of it. All the previous work can be wasted if the show is given in a careless, slovenly manner. Always have your projector lined up and *focused* before the audience comes into the room. Have the chairs arranged, and have the films ready to hand in the correct order.

Do not rewind the films and keep the audience waiting during the show. Run through your whole programme, and then rewind all the films after the audience has gone.

If you can arrange a " dimming " control for your lights and " effect " lights on the screen, so much the better, but these things are incidental and subordinate. The important things are : a screen which is properly filled with a picture that is bright enough, but not *too bright*; an audience comfortably seated in correct relationship to the screen; and a smoothly run, trouble-free programme. If enough light is available, the best screen of all is a pure white one. Silver and bead screens give much more brilliant pictures, provided that the audience is seated in a long, narrow lane between the projector and the screen.

More pictures are spoiled by having too much light in the projector than by not having enough. Do not, because it happens to be the most expensive, purchase or attempt to use in your home a projector which has been designed to function in very much larger surroundings, where its high power is really needed.

CARE OF APPARATUS

Movie apparatus is precision made, and should be looked after with care. It will respond splendidly to a regular cleaning periodically, to moderate oiling, and careful storage in a dry place.

CARE OF FILMS

Films will deteriorate unless looked after. When making joins, the minimum reasonable quantity of fresh cement should be used, as an excess will spoil the film.

The gate of the projector should be kept thoroughly clean and free from accumulated " corns " of film emulsion.

When not being projected, the film should be protected from dust and any tendency to dry out and become brittle by being stored in an air-tight can, preferably one of the humidor type. Humidor cans have a pad which is moistened with water or one of the proprietary " humidifying " fluids, and keep the film supple.

CHAPTER XIII

ARTIFICIAL-LIGHT PHOTOGRAPHY

IT has long been customary for the amateur photographer to put his camera away when " the photographic season ended " at the close of summer. Such a procedure was understandable in even somewhat recent times, when film was less sensitive, and particularly so to artificial light. But in these days film has so greatly improved that the argument no longer applies. Modern film makes indoor photography possible and simple without the need for elaborate or expensive accessories.

SUITABLE FILM

Artificial light used for home photography, however brilliant it may appear, is very much redder than daylight. Fortunately panchromatic films and plates are sensitive to all the colours of the spectrum so that they may be used with this kind of light. Increases in the speeds of the various types of emulsion which are available now enable pictures to be taken at home in the evening, without difficulty and with a measure of assured success. Super-speed panchromatic film is particularly sensitive to the redness of artificial light and therefore very suitable for snapshots with little more than the normal room lighting.

Most of the well-known photographic material manufacturers list one or more varieties of such high-speed panchromatic films and they, and the lamp makers, provide excellent data about lighting and recommended exposures for interior scenes, family groups and portraits.

SUITABLE LIGHT SOURCES

Some form of electric lighting will be found most suitable where it is available.

Gas-filled, incandescent electric lamps of the normal domestic type (for convenience they will hereafter be referred to as tungsten lamps) are very suitable. The ordinary power lamps in the domestic fittings can be replaced temporarily by others of higher wattages. 150-watt lamps will be found suitable, as these are the largest size normally equipped with bayonet caps, which will fit ordinary holders.

500-watt lamps in special lighting units are also obtainable. These are generally over-run to a slight degree.

Photoflood lamps are particularly suitable and economical. A so-called " photoflood " lamp is a normal, gas-filled, tungsten lamp which is over-run to a considerable degree. Electric lamps are normally made to burn to a given " colour-temperature "—*i.e.*, a certain pressure or voltage of supply will cause them to burn at a predetermined temperature, and thus to glow to a pre-

determined brilliance and colour. This glow is
due to heat caused by the resistance of the wire
to the passage of the electric current, and if we
increase the pressure—*i.e.*, if we, for example, put
250 volts through a lamp normally constructed
for use on a 200 volts circuit—the heat will be
much greater, and under extreme pressure the
wire will melt or burn out. If the pressure is not
too great, however, the lamp wire will glow much
more vigorously than normal, but the " life " of
the lamp will be considerably shortened. A
normal domestic tungsten lamp will burn for
approximately 1000 hours before becoming useless,
and is said to have a " life " of 1000 hours. A
photoflood lamp has a life of about two hours,
but as in practice it is only switched on for a few
moments at a time, this is of little consequence,
and the total useful life is adequate for a considerable amount of photography.   On the other hand,
over-running enables much more lighting power
for photographic purposes to be obtained from a
single lighting unit.   As an example, one of the
small 275-watt photoflood bulbs has a photographic value equivalent to a normal 750-watt
tungsten bulb.

It will thus be seen that the photoflood bulb
permits a greater total output of light to be
obtained from a given current supply.   In every
correct lighting circuit there is a fuse which,
simply explained, is a short piece of wire which
will not carry quite so much current as the main

part of the wiring without melting under the
strain. It thus ensures that if a circuit is over-
loaded by having too much current flowing through
it, the breakdown will occur in a place that is
easily accessible, and the danger from fire will also
be minimised. Connecting lamps to a lighting
circuit might almost be likened to turning on a
series of taps. The more taps that are turned on,
the greater the flow of water. The larger the
number of lamps, the greater the flow of electricity, until a point is reached when the current
flow is becoming too great, and the fuse blows out.
It is therefore desirable to ascertain how many
lighting points are connected to a particular fuse,
and what flow of current can safely pass through
the fuse or, as it is more generally stated, what
" load " the circuit will take. You can do the
former by turning off the main current, removing
one fuse, and then, after switching on the main
current, ascertaining which of your lighting points
are no longer supplied with current. The older
type of installation was provided with fuses in
pairs, but more modern ones may have only one
fuse per circuit. Pull out one fuse at a time to
locate the faulty circuit.

The permissible load on a circuit is measured in
amperes. In flats and in many houses the domestic lighting circuits are designed to carry 5
amperes, and in some cases 10 amperes. If you
have a power circuit in your house, it will generally carry at least 15 amperes. These facts will

be stated on the meter or fuse box, or can be ascertained from the electric light company.

The total number of amperes which will flow through a circuit to supply a given number of lamps can be ascertained by first adding together the stated wattage of the lamps, and then making the following simple calculation based on Ohm's law :—

$$\text{Amperes} = \frac{\text{Watts}}{\text{Volts}}.$$

For example, suppose you are using one 500-watt unit and four 100-watt units on a 200-volt circuit, the calculation would be

$$\frac{500 \text{ plus } 400 \text{ (watts)}}{200 \text{ (volts)}} = \frac{900}{200} = 4\cdot5 \text{ amperes.}$$

It would thus be quite safe to run all these lamps from an ordinary 5-ampere household circuit, but if further lights were required, another circuit would have to be used to accommodate them.

At this point, to save any possible confusion, it should be explained that the lamps you use, including photoflood lamps, should be marked with the same voltage as your own supply circuit. The " over-running " of the photoflood lamps, which was explained earlier in the chapter, is allowed for in the design of the lamps, which also includes a safety-fuse inside the lamp-base. You can, however, obtain a photoflood effect by running an ordinary tungsten lamp on a circuit of higher voltage than that for which it is rated, but you will have to work out the gain in light for yourself.

TWO IMPORTANT ELECTRICAL TIPS

NEVER strengthen an electric fuse—*i.e.*, never put in a wire which will carry more current than the proper fuse wire. Otherwise serious and expensive breakdowns, possibly followed by fire, may occur in your electric circuits.

When fitting plugs and sockets to the leads of electric lighting units, ALWAYS put the female fitting (lamp-holder or socket) on the " live " side from which the supply is being taken, and the male fitting (bayonet plug, two-pin or three-pin plug) on the lead belonging to the lamp unit itself. This avoids grave possibility of danger from accidental shock. *Whenever possible* use a three-pin plug and socket power supply, in conjunction with a three-wire cable, properly attaching the third (earth) wire to the casing of the lighting unit and the third pin of the plug. This provides additional protection.

FLASH-BULBS AND ELECTRONIC-FLASH

The expendable type of flash bulb (used once only) is similar in appearance to an ordinary electric lamp, but it is filled with fine wire or shredded-foil which burns brilliantly when ignited by the burning of a fine filament when the latter is connected to a small battery. In the smaller type of bulb a combustible paste is sometimes used instead of wire or foil, ignited in the same way. Instead of a simple battery a capacitor may be charged from a miniature 22½- or 30-volt battery and the stored energy used to burn out the ignition filament. The " flash " lasts about one seventy-fifth of a second.

The electronic flash bulb (repeating flash) consists of a relatively narrow bore quartz or glass tube filled with the rare gas xenon, through which a pulse of electrical energy is discharged from a capacitor. The working voltage may be from 250 to as high as 2,750 volts, and the flash duration from one-thousandth to one-ten-thousandth of a second.

Equipments embodying either type of bulb may be arranged to flash in synchronism with the opening of the camera shutter, either by means of internal contacts in the camera or in the shutter itself or by external " synchronisers " attached to the shutter.

DESIGNED LIGHTING UNITS

The simplest form of reflector, used with photoflood bulbs, is a cone of white card or sheet aluminium. Other more elaborate conical or hemispherical spun reflectors are also available on stands or supports which facilitate their exact placing in relation to the subject, but an old flexible lampstand will often serve the same purpose.

Newer types of lamp incorporate an internal mirror coating so that they may be used alone without an external reflector: in this instance the lampholder may be mounted on a simple bracket or clip.

The 500-watt tungsten units of the over-run type, usually referred to as "flood" lamps, are in bowl-shaped or matt-white reflectors, while yet another type has shallow matt aluminium bowl reflectors.

TYPES OF LIGHTING

The above lamps, with the exception of certain individual makes with polished reflectors, are known as flood-lamps. The light they emit is broad and general in effect, and does not throw definite hard-lined shadows. They are excellent for general work and portraiture.

The bright reflector lamps throw a slightly harder shadow and give harder, more brilliant lighting.

For really hard directional lighting a spot-light is used, and when the photographer has passed beyond the beginner stage he is strongly advised to acquire some form of spot-light unit. He does not need such an accessory for his earlier work, however. The function of the spot-light is to place a small patch or area of really intense high-light exactly on that part of the subject where the photographer requires it. It is also used to secure the "back-lit" effect which is so popular in film-play photography. A spot-light can bring a sparkle to a photograph which is unobtainable in any other way.

DISTANCE, POWER AND EXPOSURE

The exact exposure required for a given power of light depends on a variety of factors. It can be affected by the type and design of the reflector, the distance of the lamp from the subject, the colour of the subject, the colour of the surroundings, the angle of the light in relation to the camera.

The distance of the lamp from the subject has a profound effect on the brilliance of illumination, and provides an important means of controlling the " modelling " or variation of lighting in your picture.

If we consider a source of light unassisted by a reflector, placed, say, 3 feet from a subject, and then move the light back until it is 6 feet from the subject, the illumination on the subject will have fallen to one-quarter of its original power. The law is that illumination varies inversely as the square of the distance. In the above example we move the light to twice the distance, so that the power of illumination became equal to $\frac{1}{2 \times 2} = \frac{1}{4}$ of the original power of illumination. Conversely, by moving the light in to 12 inches, which is one-third the distance, the power of illumination would have become $\frac{3 \times 3}{1} = \frac{9}{1} = 9$ times the original power of illumination. It will thus be seen that merely moving the light in and out gives great flexibility of control.

This rule is upset to some extent by the use of reflectors, but the effect is very little in the case of the soft, flood-light type of reflector, while with the spot-light it hardy applies at all, owing to the action of the spot-light in concentrating or spreading the light-patch over any desired area within wide limits, whatever the distance the light-source may be from the subject.

Illumination is *not* affected to any appreciable extent by the distance of the camera from the subject. It is, however, affected very much by the lens aperture used and the time of exposure, and also by the speed of the film stock. This sounds complex, but only because for the moment we are dealing with all the possible variables. The makers of both film stock and lighting units are willing to provide fairly exact data, and several manufacturers publish excellent booklets and charts showing proposed arrangements of lighting and the correct exposure times with various films.

Merely as a very general guide, I print some characteristic figures below :—

One 275-watt photoflood in reflector, 3 feet from a fairly light subject, using a Supersensitive type of film, 1/25th of a second at f/5·6.

One 500-watt tungsten lamp in reflector, slightly over-run, 3 feet from similar subject, using a Supersensitive type of film, 1/25th of a second at f/3·5.

Photoflash lamps are very much more powerful. A typical exposure, using Supersensitive Panchromatic film, with medium-type flash-bulb in reflector at 25 feet from the subject, is f/6·5. The exposure time is controlled by the period of burning of the light, and is 1/75th of a second, but may be shortened if a synchronised flash-gun is used.

These figures apply when the light is shone fairly directly on the front of the subject. If the light-source is to the side, the exposure may have to be increased by as much as 100 per cent., depending on whether the surroundings of the subject are light or dark.

LIGHTING TECHNIQUE

When lighting a subject, take daylight conditions as your model. Remember that the sun is generally above you, even at the ends of the day, and a light which is slightly falling downwards will almost always give a pleasant effect. Again, in out-of-doors lighting there will be some reflection into the shadows from objects opposite to the direction of the sun, which will make those shadows luminous and full of detail. This effect can be accomplished in artificial light either by placing a secondary lamp more or less opposite the main one, but at a greater distance, or by employing a large white reflecting surface to pick up some of the light and play it back into the shadows.

Remember the remarks on daylight photography, and avoid direct frontal lighting. 45-degree lighting is much the safest technique for the beginner. Pay attention to your background. It should always be lit sufficiently well to give some exposure on the negative, and if several lights are being used, see that they do not throw conflicting shadows on the background. This can be avoided by bringing your model forward from the backing. On the other hand, you can build up an interesting pattern of shadows and pools of light on an otherwise plain backing, and remove flatness and monotony from your pictures. Study the work of master painters and photographers in the various galleries and exhibitions and you will receive plenty of inspiration.

CHAPTER XIV

CHEMICALS AND FORMULAE

THE MAKERS' FORMULAE

EVERY reputable manufacturer issues instructions showing the composition of the developers which he recommends with his materials, the correct fixing solution, and sometimes also formulae for after-treatment. In many cases these instructions are packed with the material, and they can always be obtained on request.

The formulae are carefully compiled by the manufacturers after a long series of tests, and are calculated to bring out the best results from materials the characteristics and requirements of which are well known to them. It is thus logical that the worker should use these formulae in preference to all others.

From time to time you will see published formulae from other sources, which are claimed, for a variety of reasons, to be improvements on the standard formulae. While I do not suggest that this is never the case, and while it may be true that such formulae give better results in the hands of their compilers, such claims should be accepted with caution, as in many cases they are arrived at after a relatively small number of experiments, and conclusions are reached under conditions which would certainly not be considered conclusive in the laboratories of the manufacturers.

STANDARD FORMULAE

There are, however, certain general purpose solutions which, while they may not give the very last atom of quality with *every* product, do give reliable results with the majority of them. For your guidance specimen formulae of these are printed below, and may be used by you for the purposes indicated.

The fixing-baths described may be used with practically all negative material and gas-light and bromide papers. Some special papers, however, call for certain modifications, which will be set forth in the instruction sheets accompanying the packages.

GOLDEN RULE

ALWAYS READ THE MAKERS' INSTRUCTION SHEETS FIRST, even when using for the first time a new grade of a material with which you are already familiar, and most certainly when you try a new manufacturer's products for the first time.

STANDARD FORMULAE

Instructions for Mixing.—The ingredients should be introduced in the order given in the formulae. Each chemical *must* be dissolved before the next one is added. The chemicals in the developer formulae should be dissolved in warm water of the quantity mentioned in the first lines of the formulae, the temperature being about 125° Fahrenheit (52° Centigrade). The final addition of cold water to bring the total volume of solution up to the quantity mentioned in the last line of the formula will also bring the solution near to the working temperature.

Stir while solution is taking place, and preferably filter the solution before use. An excellent form of filter is a funnel of glass or bakelite with a pad of cotton wool in the bottom of the cone of the funnel. Filter-papers are rather slow in action and are not necessary.

Hypo should be dissolved by suspending it in a bag or pocket of cheesecloth or similar material at the top of a glass or pottery jug, and pouring hot water on it from a kettle. As the hypo dissolves it will automatically lower the temperature of the solution.

Check the temperatures of all solutions before using them.

Average Negative Developer.

(NOT suitable for 35-mm. miniature films.)

M.Q. (METOL-HYDROQUINONE) CARBONATE.

	Avoirdupois.	Metric.
Water (warm) . . .	30 ounces	850 ml.
Metol	16 grains	1 gram
Sodium sulphite (crystals) .	3 ounces	85 grams
Hydroquinone. . .	70 grains	4·5 ,,
Sodium carbonate (crystals) .	2 ounces	57 ,,
Potassium bromide . .	25 grains	1·6 ,,
Solution made up with cold water to total volume of . .	40 ounces	1 litre

The above is a WORKING SOLUTION, which means that it is used exactly in the form in which it is prepared according to the formula, and without further dilution.

It should be used at a temperature not lower than 65° Fahrenheit (18° Centigrade), and not higher than 70° Fahrenheit (21° Centigrade). Average development time, for medium speed negative plates or films, six minutes.

Average Paper Developer (for Gas-light and Bromide Paper)

M.Q. (METOL-HYDROQUINONE) CARBONATE.

	Avoir-dupois.	Metric.
Water (warm) . . .	30 ounces	850 ml.
Metol	30 grains	2 grams
Sodium sulphite (crystals) .	2 ounces	57 ,,
Hydroquinone . . .	115 grains	7·5 ,,
Sodium carbonate (crystals) .	3 ounces	85 ,,
Potassium bromide .	30 grains	2 ,,
Solution made up with cold water to total volume of .	40 ounces	1 litre

The above is a STOCK SOLUTION, which means that it is made up in concentrated form for storage, but must be diluted for some purposes.

For GAS-LIGHT paper it is used at full strength. Average development time : 30 seconds to 1 minute at normal temperature, according to make of paper.

For BROMIDE paper 1 volume of solution is diluted with an equal volume of water (*i.e.*, 1 ounce of water to 1 ounce of stock solution).

Average development time, at 65° Fahrenheit (18° Centigrade), 1½ to 2 minutes, according to make of paper.

Note.—For CHLORO-BROMIDE papers it is better to use the formula and time recommended by the maker of the paper.

Acid Fixing Bath, for plates, films, gas-light and bromide papers.

	Avoirdupois.	Metric.
Hypo (sodium thiosulphate) .	8 ounces	227 grams
Water (hot) . . .	40 ounces	1 litre
Add when cool potassium meta-bisulphite. . . .	1 ounce	28·5 grams

Note.—Use at 65° Fahrenheit (18° Centigrade).

Plain Fixing Bath.

	Avoirdupois.	Metric.
Hypo (sodium thiosulphate) .	4 ounces	113 grams
Water (hot)	40 ounces	1 litre

Note.—Use at 65° Fahrenheit (18° Centigrade).

This is sufficient for 50 quarter-plate (4¼″ × 3¼″) prints.

SOME PHOTOGRAPHIC CHEMICALS

The list which follows by no means represents the total number of chemicals which are obtainable and usable in photography. I have listed only those with which the beginner is likely to come in contact, and about which he should therefore know something.

Developing Agents.

Amidol (di-aminophenol-hydrochloride).	White or bluish-grey crystals, very soluble in water. Affected by light and air—goes black. Does not keep long in solution.	Used with sodium sulphite as a bromide paper developer.
Hydroquinone (*p* dihydroxy-benzene).	Long, needle-like, white crystals. Moderately soluble in water.	Builds up density, and is used both alone and also in conjunction with metol. Needs an accelerator. Becomes useless at temperature below 65° Fahr.
Metol (mono-methyl para-mino-phenol sulphate.	Pearly-white powder of very fine crystals.	Gives fine detail, and average density. Used either alone or with hydroquinone. Needs accelerator.
Pyro., pyro-gallol, abbreviation of pyrogallic acid (trihydr-oxybenzene).	There are two forms : (1) Very fine flaky powder, which is liable to fly around the workroom and cause trouble ; (2) Crystals. Both are extremely soluble in water.	Once very popular, but now less so. Give an image which is a combination of silver deposit and stain.
Quinol.	Another name for hydroquinone, *q.v.*	

Preservatives.

Sodium sulphite (must not be confused with sodium sulphide).	Can be obtained in two forms : (1) Crystals (white) which should be clear and clean ; (2) White powder. This has twice the strength of the crystal form for a given weight.	Used to prevent the developing agents in a solution from becoming oxidised and discoloured.

Preservatives.

Potassium metabisulphite.	Colourless crystals with a slight acid smell.	Used both for developer and fixing baths, to resist oxidisation and discoloration.
Sodium bisulphite.	Can be obtained in two forms : (1) Solid crystals. (2) In liquid form, when it is known as bisulphite lye.	Used as a preservative in conjunction with sodium sulphite for pyro. developers. Also used in fixing baths.

Accelerators.

Borax (sodium borate).	A pure white powder of very fine crystals.	A mild agent, used in fine grain developers.
Potassium carbonate.	A granular white powder, which rapidly picks up water if not kept well sealed.	Similar characteristics to sodium carbonate, *q.v.*
Sodium carbonate.	Can be obtained in two forms : (1) Colourless crystals, small and irregular in form; (2) The desiccated or anhydrous form. Coarse white powder. Has $2\frac{3}{4}$ times the strength of the crystal form for a given weight.	The most frequently used accelerator, for both plate and paper developers.

Restrainer.

Potassium bromide.	Small-sized white crystals, fairly regular in form.	Prevents unduly rapid action of the developer, and preserves the clarity of the lighter tones in both negative and print.

Fixing Agents.

Hypo., hyposulphite of soda (sodium thiosulphate).	Colourless, hexagonal crystals. Very soluble in water.	Dissolves away the unwanted sensitive silver salts in a developed negative or print without affecting the metallic silver image.

Note.—Potassium metabisulphite and sodium bisulphite are not in themselves fixing agents, but are used as preservatives in the fixing bath. (*See under* Preservatives.)

Hardening Agents.

Alum, potassium. Alum, ammonium.	Both are obtainable in large, clear crystals. Fairly soluble in water.	Used in fixing bath. They harden the negative or print by tanning the gelatine.
Alum, chrome.	Large violet crystals, the solution normally appearing green.	Used either in the fixing bath, or as a separate bath after fixing. When fresh has much stronger action than either potassium or ammonium alum.
Formalin.	A 40 per cent. solution of formaldehyde (a gas) in water. Strong, sharp smell.	Used much diluted. An extremely powerful hardener, but somewhat unpleasant to use.

CHAPTER XV

FUTURE WORK

THE VALUE OF READING

THIS volume is a general outline of the simple principles of photographic practice, and because it has touched on a wide range of subjects, its treatment of each of them has necessarily been general. I hope, however, it has prompted a desire on your part to learn more about this most interesting of all pursuits.

Much can be learned by regular reading of the excellent photographic periodicals which are published, and this will also serve to keep you up to date with the latest developments of the hobby. In the pages of such publications the manufacturers advertise their newest goods; advanced workers describe their experiments with new products and new processes; the questions of some readers are answered by the inquiry departments of the magazines for the benefit of all readers; the work of readers is criticised. A list of periodicals is given below.

You will also find much help in reading other books on photography which are more advanced than this one, and especially those volumes which are devoted to particular branches of it.

The list printed on page 188 should help you in making your choice of the right books to study.

JOIN A PHOTOGRAPHIC SOCIETY

I would also recommend to you the wisdom of joining your local photographic society. There you will meet other enthusiasts who are working on the same lines as yourself. By mutually discussing mistakes and disappointments you can help each other to avoid many of them. A casual word or comment from a better-informed fellow-member will often save you unnecessary experiment and expenditure. Direct comparison of your own work with that of others will inspire you to do better yourself, and will often encourage you by showing you that your own work is better than you had imagined it to be. The various lectures and demonstrations arranged by the society will give you intimate contact with the latest developments in materials and processes and their possibilities. You will enjoy the photographic outings and the social gatherings. In a brief while you will be able to enjoy the opportunities to enter competitions organised by your own society, and you may later send entries to the national and international photographic competitions. Then as you progress you can consider joining the national body, *The Royal Photographic Society*. There is a peculiar satisfaction in seeing your name in the catalogue of an exhibition organised on the other side of the world. Pictures speak every language.

BIBLIOGRAPHY

PHOTOGRAPHIC PERIODICALS

Weekly.

Amateur Photographer.
Iliffe and Sons, Ltd., Dorset House, Stamford Street, London, S.E.1.   Popular and general interest.

The British Journal of Photography.
H. Greenwood and Co., Ltd., 24 Wellington Street, Strand, London, W.C.2.   Technical and professional interest.

Monthly

35 mm. Photography.

Colour Photography.

Amateur Movie-Maker.

Amateur Cine World.
Fountain Press, 46–47, Chancery Lane, London, W.C.2.   These magazines are of popular and general interest.

The Photographic Journal.

The Journal of Photographic Science.
These journals are the official organs of The Royal Photographic Society, 16 Princes Gate, Kensington, London, S.W.7.   Available by subscription, but issued free to all members of the Society.

Annual.

The British Journal Photographic Almanac.
Published by **The British Journal of Photography.** Contains informative articles, a pictorial section and many technical and other references.

Photograms of the Year.
Published by the **Amateur Photographer.**   An international review of pictorial photography.

BOOKS

ELEMENTARY

The Gevaert Manual of Photography.

The Ilford Manual of Photography.

How to Make Good Pictures.   Kodak, Ltd.

Most manufacturers issue leaflets and booklets, either without charge or at small cost, which it is well worth collecting to provide the basis of a reference library.

INTERMEDIATE

Photography Today.   Dr. D. A. Spencer.

Photography.   Dr. C. E. K. Mees.

Panchromatism.   Ilford, Ltd.

Wratten Light Filters.   Kodak, Ltd.

Dictionary of Photography.   Iliffe and Sons, Ltd.

ADVANCED

Photography : Its Principles and Practice.   C. B. Neblette, F.R.P.S.

Photography : Theory and Practice.   L. P. Clerc, Hon. F.R.P.S.

The Theory of the Photographic Process.   Dr. C. E. K. Mees.

PHOTOGRAPHIC PUBLISHING HOUSES

The Focal Press, Ltd., 51 Fitzroy Square, London, W.1.

The Fountain Press, Ltd., 46–47 Chancery Lane, London, W.C.2.

The above very short list by no means exhausts the total literature on the subject of photography and its many branches, and the reader is advised to visit his local library, where he will generally find a book list on the subject. A visit to a good photographic dealer is also worth while, as many dealers carry quite large stocks of books from which a selection may be made to build a personal library : however, choose with discretion so that your books match your growing knowledge of the art or the science of this fascinating subject.

INDEX

A